A MIRACLE
ON THE ROAD TO
RECOVERY

a true story

A MIRACLE
ON THE ROAD TO
RECOVERY

a true story

JOHN KELLER
WITH MARGIE KNIGHT

WORD & SPIRIT
RESOURCES
Tulsa, Oklahoma

A Miracle on the Road to Recovery
By John Keller

ISBN: 978 1 936314 99 7 51499

Published and distributed by: Word & Spirit Resources
                               P.O. Box 701403
                               Tulsa, OK 74170

Writer/ Publishing & Design Director: Margie Knight
                                       KnightWriter-2-Publish
                                       Email: knightwriter2publish@gmail.com

Cover Design: Marcus Buckner
                   www.visualintake.com

Interior Design: Joy Kusek
                   Email: joykusek@gmail.com

Back cover photo by: Ann Westerman

Worldwide Distribution
Printed in Canada

This Book
Is Dedicated
To Our Sons,
Caden and Dalton

"Daddy's Home!"

We Love You,
Daddy & Mommy

Acknowledgements

From John, April, Jan & James Keller

First of all we want to thank our Lord and Savior Jesus Christ for being with us and guiding us each step of the way through this storm in our lives. We saw His hand everywhere along the road during John's recovery.

Our family is a family of faith. We never gave up and pushed on believing and praising God for each miraculous intervention and manifestation of healing in John's life day by day. We watched for divine connections along the way and took every opportunity to minister to everyone that crossed our path. We knew John would want us to do it.

We were blessed beyond measure by the way the office staff at the family business pulled together and picked up the extra load while John was not there. We appreciate how the managers and workers in the stores went the extra mile each and every day to maintain the level of excellence John instilled in everyone. Your prayers and loving support made a difference in our lives during all those months. We are especially grateful to Patti Kohrt Munoz who spent countless hours compiling and organizing all the documents and material for the book and, also, for the DVD's, that Patti and her husband, John, created and have now posted on You Tube. We, also, cherish the time our daughters, Jennifer Keller Majors and Jené Keller Byrom, spent establishing and maintaining the blog site throughout John's journey into wholeness.

We want to take this opportunity to acknowledge and thank April's family members, who walked through many difficult months and gave sacrificially to help with the boys and to hold up April's arms and encourage her heart as she stood strong beside John and traveled back and forth between Houston and McAllen.

We are so grateful for all the brothers and sisters in the Lord that we have known all these years and those we came to know during this time that selflessly ministered to all of us through visits in the hospital and at home, phone calls, emails, text messages, scriptures given to confirm other words, prayers lifted up, food delivered, baby sitting, and even to giving of their own furniture for the apartment in Houston, as well as being led by the Holy Spirit to give monetarily when we needed help. We can never say thank you enough to all of you, worldwide, who were so obedient to continue praying and standing in the gap for John's complete healing.

We are so appreciative of all the doctors, nurses, medical techs, therapists, hospital staff, administrators, social workers, ambulance drivers, EMTs and any others that obey the call to caringly minister healing and/or support to the sick or injured and their loved ones.

Table of Contents

Foreword

by Chuck D. Pierce

Prayer is a wonderful privilege that we have been given. Mere man can commune with Holy God. This opens our hearts and minds to SEE in ways that we could never SEE in the natural realm. We are greatly privileged when God allows us to pray for one of His children. This book reveals the privilege that God gave many to pray for a young man named John Keller.

One Sunday morning while leading corporate prayer, the Lord spoke to me and said, "Watch what I can do." He then took His Finger and went deep into John Keller's brain and began to rearrange, reconnect, and heal parts that only He could touch.

God is a covenant God and develops that same understanding in His children who follow Him. Covenant is a word that has the meaning of alignment, agreement, and oneness all wrapped up in relationship. Covenant is a God-word that means we first must *agree* that He is and *believe* that He loves us. Next, we must agree that His Son came to redeem us. In this agreement, we yield our life to life in the Son and receive His Spirit into our heart. Once we experience this and adhere to His life, we receive all the blessings that He has for us in heavenly places. Additionally, the Lord has covenant with the land. Therefore, we have covenant with His land. We are His covenant stewards. Our role is to watch after, cultivate, and steward His plan of fullness for the earth that He created. I call this vertical covenantal alignment.

The next type of covenant is *horizontal covenant*. He made us and positioned us in the body of Christ, so we need each other. He then positions people on our path that are covenant friends. John 15:13 NKJV says, *"Greater love has no one than this, than to lay down one's life for his friends."* James and Jan Keller have been covenant friends of mine and Pam's for over 30 years. During that time, we have had almost a dozen kids between us and had many more live in our homes. Covenant also means that you do not have to fight your wars by yourself. If you are in battle, those in covenant with you go to battle on your behalf. We have warred through financial crises, sickness, deaths of friends, ministry issues, and so many other wars, the pages of this book could not contain.

However, when James called and said, ***"John (their 33-year-old son) has been in a motorcycle accident, and the prognosis is not good,"*** I knew that this war was greater than what we had experienced in the past. *A Miracle on the Road to Recovery* is about the war for life and not letting go until you *see* victory. John Keller and Margie Knight have captured in these pages what is necessary to fight the good fight of faith and win. This book demonstrates the miracle of prayer; the gift of faith, friends and family; and the supernatural hand of God. This book is a miracle! This book is faith in action!

My wife recently made this incredible statement: *"Expecting the miraculous is one of the childlike characteristics that have to be cultivated and protected in a world full of cynicism and disappointment."*

Miracles and faith must go hand-in-hand. Faith is related to every part of our Christian lives. *By faith* we receive salvation (see Eph. 2:8-9). Faith is associated with our experiences of sanctification (see Acts 26:18), purification (see Acts 15:9), justification (see Rom. 4:5; 5:1), and adoption (see Gal. 3:26; Col. 3:24). All are dependent upon our faith.

Faith comes by hearing — hearing by the Word of the Lord! There is a war of faith to hear, stand firm, and enter into at times if we are to see our promises manifest. This book presents both the war and the triumph.

The word MIRACLE is linked with the principle of WONDER! Miracles are the wonderful events that only God can conceive in heaven and that we see in earth. Miracles are supernatural manifestations of divine power in this atmospheric world in which we live where special revelations of the presence and power of God are displayed. All natural events become subservient and aid His power from the Throne Room as released in and through us here in the earth realm. Once His power is released, He establishes and preserves His will and the life processes of human flesh in the world. A miracle, or His power, extends eternity into the atmosphere where we live and walk.

This power aligns with the "the Spirit of the Lord" so the "the Finger of God" (Luke 4:18; 11:20; cf. Acts 3:12) **can work.** Miracles are "powers," "mighty works," "wonderful works," and "manifestations of the power of God." He uses His Finger to touch, paint, and work His will like the mighty Molder of Life that He is! He creates a new order out of a mess. He enters the natural laws of earth and redirects their actions. The supernatural finger of God rearranges the natural world. The whole world is filled with wonders to him who has eyes to see. The natural world everywhere is full of marvels, but we must look for the Finger that makes the natural wondrous and alive with GOD. That is what we have here: an account of the natural becoming alive with the Holy — the normal filled with the Wonder-Working Author of the beginning and end of our faith.

A miracle is not only wonderful but has the sense of being a "new thing!" This new thing awakens us to a Divine Power that our eyes were unable to see. John Keller's motorcycle accident awakened all of those in covenant alignment with the Kellers to the wonder that only God can produce: Jan, John's mother, with her unshakeable faith; James, his dad, with struggles to stand, representing the power of God working in the midst of a normal family; John's wife, April, his sisters, as well as his extended family and friends, experiencing and responding to a tragic, natural moment that created a supernatural event. It is all recorded here. This is one of those modern accounts Jesus talks about as being "the greater works" that we would see as we followed after Him.

Miracles belong to the higher order that is recognized in this account. His Finger and working power has an appropriate place in the great plan and purpose of lives that have been knitted together in Him. Miracles produce revelation. What we could not normally see, we now see!

Faith sees when miracles happen! Faith was one of the main thrusts of Jesus' ministry. In the Gospels, we continually find statements such as, "Your *faith* has healed you." In Jesus' hometown, He could not do mighty miracles because the people there lacked faith. He wasn't powerless to do so, but the atmosphere in that place prevented our Lord from exhibiting the power of faith. However, whenever He found men and women of faith, He released His power, and miracles took place. God assures us that *if we believe,* then nothing is impossible, and He withholds nothing.

The Bible teaches that if we can *enter into* faith and *stay in* faith, everything else will come (see Matt. 8:13; 15:28; Mark 9:23). I don't care what we face in life, if we can move into a position of faith and stay there, we will walk in victory on a day-to-day basis. The Greek word for faith is *pistis.* It means to have trust or confidence. When we walk in faith, we trust and demonstrate confidence in God in the midst of our situation. Jesus' call to "have faith in God" (Mark 11:22) was an exhortation to enter into a trusting commitment to the Father in the midst of whatever we might face. When Jesus said, "Your faith has made you whole," He was teaching that *confidence in* or *allegiance to* God releases God's wholeness into our lives.

Faith is not static. It is the dynamic interaction of our spirit man with God. We have each been given a measure of faith through the hearing of the Word (see Rom. 10:17). As we walk with the Lord, we are exhorted to increase our faith by living our faith (see Rom. 1:17). God wants us to put on faith (see 1 Thess. 5:8), to grow in faith (see 2 Cor. 10:15), and to have a steadfast faith (see 1 Cor. 15:58) that becomes a strong faith (see Rom. 4:19-20).

Faith is a fruit of the Holy Spirit (see Gal. 5:22). There is also a spiritual gift of faith (see 1 Cor. 12:8-9). In times of need, the Holy Spirit can release to us a greater measure of faith. However, unless our shield of faith is in place, we cannot see all of these dimensions of faith activated.

This book demonstrates faith! *"Now faith is the assurance (the confirmation, the title deed) of the things [we] hope for, being the proof of things [we] do not see and the conviction of their reality [faith perceiving as real fact what is not revealed to the senses]"* (Heb. 11:1, *AMP*). What an incredible statement! In the midst of today's tumultuous world, faith becomes the most important issue. It is vital to understand this aspect of our spiritual lives, yet there is so much confusion over it. Verse 2 of Hebrews 11, which is often called the faith chapter, holds a key: "For by [faith] the elders obtained a good testimony." These saints obtained a good reputation because they actively expressed their relationship with a holy God. Their personal holiness is not what they are known for in history; they are known because they trusted in, relied on, and interacted with the God of the universe.

The elders *used* their faith. We must grasp this concept if we are to raise our shield of faith. We must know the same God that these witnesses knew. We cannot have an effective faith without understanding the dedication and relationship that those who have gone before us displayed. They show us how we can be victorious in the midst of, and in spite of, the circumstances that surround us.

Jesus healed sick people and worked miracles. He said that those who believe would do the same. He dealt with many organic causes of illness and individuals affected by madness, birth defects, and infections. The blind, the deaf, the lame, and others who suffered approached Him for help. I especially love the story of the woman with the spirit of infirmity who "pressed through" in Mark 5:25-34. She is an incredible example of personal overcoming. She overcame the religious structure of the day, the reproach of being a woman, and the stigma of being unclean. She pressed through to touch the Lord. This caused the Lord to release "virtue" (*KJV*, "power" in the *NKJV*) from His own body that healed her condition.

Why do bad things happen in the natural world in which we live? In the Hebraic culture of the day, most people believed that illness was the direct consequence of sin (see John 9:1-3). However, Jesus shifted this concept by healing a blind man who had been sick since birth. When Jesus' disciples asked, "Who sinned, this man or his parents, that he was born blind?" Jesus answered that the sickness was not related to the man or his parents, "but that the works of God should be revealed in him" (John 9:3). Many wrong choices produce consequences that affect our body, but Jesus came to extend grace to bring us out from the bondage of the punishment of sin and into healing and wholeness. He had the power to both forgive sin and to heal (see Matt. 9:1-8; compare Mark 2:1-12; Luke 5:17-26).

On several occasions, Jesus used His own saliva as an ointment or anointing (see Mark 7:32-35; 8:22-25; John 9:6-7). I find this fascinating — one of the primary ways DNA is collected for testing is through saliva samples. Jesus took His own saliva, placed it on the eyes of the blind, and watched their eyes form. He also healed those who suffered from mental illnesses and epilepsy — sicknesses usually associated with demonic powers (see Mark 9:18). The Lord addressed issues of fever and dysentery (see Matt. 8:14-15). Sterility and barrenness were also major issues in biblical times.

Regardless of the cause of their distress, people found that Jesus was the answer to their every need. Today, the Lord addresses motorcycle accidents.

Do We Need Doctors in this miraculous process? The answer is, "Yes!" Most doctors understand cycles. Recently I wrote: "If medical doctors begin to take a biblical approach toward an individual — that of seeing the individual made whole — they will be able to find the root cause of that person's problem and not only help to heal that individual but, also, help to prevent disease in the future. With doctoral skill and advances in medicine, individuals can better reverse deficiencies that have created paths of decay. *Why do we need doctors?* Because they interject miraculous techniques and discoveries into the natural world of man with skill and precision that prolongs God's plan in an individual. They can validate what God is doing in a skeptical world."

John Keller is a miracle. This book is a miracle. I thank God for this covenant experience in which He allowed all of us to participate. Enter into this miracle as you read!

Prologue

James Keller

"Tomorrow...about this time...things are going to change!"

"Tomorrow...about this time...things are going to change!"

"Tomorrow...about this time...things are going to change!"[1]

A s the lyrical beat of the tempo and the deep resonate voice of Dr. Joseph Garlington reverberated these words through the Super Pit Coliseum at the University of North Texas, he drove home the urgency of the Lord's revelation of Job 22:28:

> *"You will also declare a thing, and it will be established for you; so light will shine on your ways."*

Our spirits were electrified with an expectancy that our lives were about to change. In what way or to what extent, we had no idea.

Jan and I were attending the "Starting the Year Off Right" Conference sponsored by Glory of Zion International in Denton, TX during the first week in January 2008. Dr. Garlington, a dynamic apostolic leader, was just one of the anointed conference speakers, but it was his uniquely captivating message that caught our attention when he said, "God will not establish what you don't decree."[2] Our dear friend and apostle, Chuck Pierce, who hosted the conference, added another important key to this revelation when he said, "Your comprehension is not a prerequisite to your cooperation."[3] In other words, if we make a decree in anticipation of an unprecedented act of God, we don't have to be concerned with "how" or "when" God will do it. He *will* establish it!

We knew it was critical that we be prepared in advance for whatever impending event or circumstance might impact our family, our business, our church body, or our nation. So, we purchased the DVD and listened to it numerous times over the next few weeks to capture the essence of declaring and decreeing what God says. Little did we know how this message would play out in our lives when just a few weeks later, in the blink of an eye, our whole family's world turned upside down.

.

Introduction

John Keller

On February 17, 2008 my life and the lives of my entire family suddenly changed forever. A beautiful sunny afternoon turned into darkness when a car struck my motorcycle and sent me spiraling 150 feet in the air across five lanes of traffic before landing on the pavement. An eye witness saw me fly end-over-end like a helicopter swirling through the air, then hit the pavement on my bottom, fall back and hit my head. I now tell people, "I didn't go to heaven or hell, I just blacked out."

This book is a testimony of how life as we knew it was instantly interrupted but through the course of two years, has been transformed into a miracle of biblical proportions. It is the hope and prayers of our family that sharing our miraculous journey on the road to recovery will show you how important it is to know God's Word and to be able to declare and decree it over your life, even when it feels like everything is out of control.

If I was writing this book alone, it would be filled with "blank pages," because for me that is exactly what this journey has been. I spent 338 days of it asleep, and so, the pages of my part of the story are blank, as depicted on the front cover. Therefore, my beautiful wife, April; my precious mom,

Jan Keller; and my wonderful dad, James Keller, will be filling in these pages for you. Some additional family members, friends and even a few medical and therapy team members will add their testimonials and comments as well.

When I woke up 338 days after the accident, I had no idea where I was. I did not recognize the lady with the British accent who was asking me questions. She told me that she was an occupational therapist and then asked me who the woman was sitting beside me. I turned to my right, looked at my mother, turned back to the occupational therapist, and said, "Mom." My voice sounded strange. It was very raspy like I had not talked in weeks, similar to when you have laryngitis. I felt different too. My body was weak. She asked me if I knew where I was. I shook my head no. She told me I was in the hospital, and what was even more amazing, that I had been there for almost a year! She said I was involved in a motorcycle accident, and I had a traumatic brain injury. This was my first conversation in 338 days.

I asked how my family was. I wanted to know about my wife, April, and my two boys, Caden and Dalton. I asked about my dad; my sisters, Jennifer and Jené, and my brother Charles. I wanted to talk with everyone. I, also, wanted to know about the family business and how it was going. I was shocked and amazed to find out that almost an entire year was gone. Then I realized I was hungry. Apparently, I had not eaten in 338 days either. My miraculous journey on the road to recovery was far from over, but waking up was where it began for me.

A sign posted over my bed read, "John Keller: Miracle in Progress," and this journey is certainly a true, modern-day miracle. For those who know and have a relationship with God the Father and those who do not, this story will inspire you to be grateful for the things you have and challenge you to change what the Lord shows you on your own journey. I am a living witness that miracles do happen, and they can happen for you as well. All it requires is faith in a living God.

> *Now faith is the substance of things hoped for, the evidence of things not seen.*
>
> Hebrews 11:1 NKJV

Often we can't always see with our eyes what is being done in the course of a miracle. So it was for my family, as they walked on the peaks and valleys of the miracle journey month after month. The miracle markers signifying progress were at times hidden or may have seemed minuscule, but each one was an important forward step of faith. You'll be surprised how many miracle markers appear in this book and continue to be manifested in my recovery to wholeness.

My family shed many tears but rejoiced in spite of difficult days, because they were encouraged and stood firm on the promises of God's Word and what He said He would do. I am convinced I would not be alive today if they hadn't fought the battle on my behalf and refused to give up. God did what He said He would do, and I now boldly testify of His goodness and grace to anyone who will listen.

Chapter 1

Life Interrupted

Jan Keller

It was Sunday, February 17, 2008. I awoke early in the morning with an urgency to pray for our family, specifically our four children, Jennifer, John, Jené and Charles, their spouses, and all nine of our grandchildren. I began praying the Armor of God, as found in Ephesians 6, over all of them.

After praying and feeling a release in my spirit, I went about our normal Sunday morning routine. Shortly thereafter, James and I headed for church. The message preached that morning was on encouragement for which I was later thankful. As we left church, I shared with James a vision I had of him and John walking into the office, and everyone was clapping as they gathered around John. I praised God for the vision, not knowing the significance of it at that time. James and I were supposed to have been in San Antonio that Sunday attending a 60th birthday celebration for a longtime friend. Just before leaving on the trip, we were notified that the birthday celebration had been called off due to illness, so we remained in town. When church was over, we went directly home.

James had decided after church that he would join John on an afternoon motorcycle ride, but James was delayed by a dead battery on his own bike. John, in the meantime, stopped at one of the family-owned stores just a couple of blocks from home to gas up his bike. James called John and tried to get him to wait there, but John said he would ride on ahead, slowly, so James could catch up with him. That opportunity never came.

What seemed like a peaceful Sunday afternoon was shattered when April called with the news that John had been in an accident. We later learned that at 1:30 pm, John was traveling north on a busy city street. Traffic was heavy as church had just been let out and all of the nearby restaurants were packed. Suddenly, John was hit by a car pulling out of a shopping center. His motorcycle was torn into three major pieces, and the rest of the bike was scattered all over the road. John was thrown 150 feet into the air across five lanes of traffic and landed back down on the pavement on his bottom in a sitting position, which fractured his pelvis into three pieces. He then fell backwards and hit his head on the asphalt, suffering a fractured skull at the back of his head on the right side. The car that hit him was totaled. John was not wearing a helmet or protective gear.

I immediately went to find James in the garage at his dad's house next door where he was trying to get his bike started to go and join John. I told him John had been in an accident, and although the reports were that it was not too bad, he was being transported to the hospital. We needed to go meet the ambulance at the hospital since April had to wait for someone to come and stay with the boys.

Our daughter, Jennifer and her family were on vacation in the Rio Grande Valley only about an hour away. They were able to get to the hospital relatively quickly. Our youngest daughter, Jené and her family, who live in McAllen, were on vacation in Dallas, and our son, Charles, resides in Dallas. They all began making their way to McAllen and arrived later in the evening.

As we drove to the hospital, I was praying and declaring and decreeing over John that he would live and fulfill God's plan for his life. The message we had heard from Dr. Joseph Garlington at the conference in January that what we decree will be established was firmly implanted in my spirit.

• • •

John Keller was a child of promise from the moment he was conceived. When our first daughter, Jennifer was two years old, James and I began praying about having a son to carry on the Keller name. We focused our prayers on Psalm 37:4 that says, *"Delight yourself also in the Lord, and He will give you the desires of your heart."*

The Lord heard and answered our prayer. To our delight, John Keller was born on December 31, 1974. It was a very difficult delivery, and when the birthing was complete, I loudly proclaimed, "Praise the Lord!" The doctor said that was the first time he had heard the Lord's name used in such a way, because he was used to hearing women curse God in the midst of their pain.

John had to be delivered with forceps so he came into this world with his first black eye and a bump on his head. He, also, had a heart murmur, but it never affected his life. John has always been a fighter and strong willed. We knew early on that we were going to have to carefully mold but not crush John's will. It was challenging at times, but we knew consistent discipline was necessary to make a difference when he was older. In kindergarten, we were told that John had learning disabilities. We declared that John would excel in his school work as we taught him self-discipline and how to focus in order to persevere in hard times.

We later had another precious daughter, Jené, and our family was complete, or so we thought. As the kids grew up, James took on the role of Youth Pastor for our church in Houston, Texas, where we lived at that time. Over the years, our family came to know and love many children that were not our own biologically. However, one special young man entered our home and our hearts one day when Charles, then 16, was introduced into and then adopted by our family permanently.

Recently, James and I watched the movie, *The Blind Side*, based on a true story of a young man who was adopted at the age of 16. We wept for joy as the story was so similar to our experience with Charles becoming part of our family.

John had physical strength and a love for sports, especially playing basketball in high school. He, also, had a passion for anything with wheels. At six years old, he started to ride motor bikes in one form or fashion.

After graduating from Texas A&M in 1998 with a Bachelor of Arts degree in marketing, John returned to McAllen to work in the family-owned business, operating gasoline/convenience stores. He loved solving business challenges and excelled in developing new strategies for business growth.

Eventually, John was named vice-president of the company and became responsible for running all 37 stores with approximately 350 employees.

John knew April Helge in high school, but they didn't date until they were in college at Texas A&M. They were married in August of 2000. John and April's oldest son, Caden, was born in November of 2005, and their second son, Dalton, was born in December of 2007, just two months before John's accident.

John never lost his love for wheels. He had a custom chopper built to his specifications to fit his 6'5"/200 pound frame. He loved to work out, so he was very strong and muscular. You could always tell when it was John going down the road on the bright orange chopper motorcycle with the blue flames. Most of the time, you could hear him before you actually saw him.

• • •

As the events at the hospital unfolded that February day, in this mother's heart, it was incomprehensible how such tragedy could have befallen our family. But I continued to encourage myself in the Lord and decree His Word, because I knew our tomorrow had come and everything was about to change. We were going to walk where we had never been before, but our God was already going before us preparing the way for John's miracle.

Just several weeks before, the hospital to which John was transported had hung a huge advertising banner on the outside of the building that among other things said, "Just Get Here!" John had seen the sign and chuckled about it a few days earlier, wondering what it meant as it seemed to be very strange statement for a hospital to display on the side of the building. As it turned out, the banner was the hospital's way of advertising itself as the first certified trauma center in McAllen. They now had operating rooms ready for patients with emergencies such as this. God was in control and already working for John's well being! Just one month earlier, these rooms would not have been ready to receive John.

The physician director of this new trauma center lives in Jerusalem. He had recently relocated his family back to Jerusalem, and he flies in to the Rio Grande Valley for fourteen days and then goes home for a period of time. On the day of John's accident, the director just happened to be in town. God was already answering prayers! We soon discovered God had, also, provided the other doctors that would be needed. The neurosurgeon and the orthopedic surgeon were on hand at the hospital.

When April arrived at the hospital, I let her know John was badly hurt and said, "We have to stand and declare that we won't go by what we *see* but by what we *know* God has promised." Then I held her in my arms and prayed for her. Over the coming months we had to remind ourselves of this declaration when so often what we saw with our eyes didn't look good. We had to stand firm on what we knew His Word said.

• • •

As you walk with us through the journey our family took for John's miracle healing, we want to help you appropriate the keys we learned along the way. Be sure to read the powerful miracle testimonies after each chapter as well.

• • •

KEYS TO WALKING OUT A MIRACLE:

1. Obey promptings from the Lord to pray.

2. Pay attention to and record dreams and visions.

3. Declare and decree out loud what God says about your situation.

4. Don't go by what you *see*, go by what you *know* God's Word promises.

Miracle Testimony

Jennifer Keller Majors

I *still vividly remember the phone call with my mom when I found out my younger brother, John, had been in an accident. We were just returning home from a weekend getaway with some close family friends. In the middle of laughing and joking with them, I called my mom to let her know we were on our way home. She answered the phone with concern and shock in her voice and said, "April, oh my gosh, are you ok?"*

I replied, "Mom, it's me, Jennifer." She then explained that she had just gotten a call from April saying John had been in an accident with his motorcycle. I knew in my heart after hearing those words, that it was not good, because John never wore a helmet. I began to pray immediately! Arriving an hour later at the hospital, it was confirmed that John had sustained injuries that might take his life.

I really can't remember if it was the next day or a few days later, but I felt I had to visit the accident site so I could see for myself exactly what we were up against. I needed to know how to pray, what to pray against, and what to ask the Lord to do specifically for John. At that very moment, seeing the accident site for the first time, I dug in my heels and decided I was going to be a prayer warrior, like never before, for John's life. Not in a million years, would I have envisioned that my husband, children, and I would still be praying daily for John and his healing two years later.

Thinking back, the most important thing I learned through this walk is to never give up. No matter what the circumstances look like, never quit, never stop, never accept defeat, and keep praying, keep asking, keep knocking, keep seeking because He does hear and He will answer. I received my personal confirmation that God was going to heal John in the drive-thru lane at Starbucks. I dropped my children off at school and headed over for my usual morning coffee. Listening to Christian music and talking to the Lord about some specifics concerning John, He confirmed in my spirit that He was working all things out for good concerning John. It was like nothing I've ever experienced before in my life. A peace came over me, and, yet, I began to weep uncontrollably. From that point on, our prayers changed. What had been requests and pleas, now became prayers of thanks for:

- *All He had done, was doing and would continue to do.*
- *A loving husband who allowed me the freedom to go help my family during this time, and for children who believed they served a God who was bigger and loved us more than I understood.*
- *The staff, therapists, doctors, nurses, and caretakers that surrounded our family daily with kindness, support and words of encouragement.*
- *Eyes to see the Lord's hand on us each step of the way and ears to hear the Lord speak words of confirmation in the most unusual ways.*
- *Family, friends, the body of Christ, and teachers who stood strong in prayer right beside us.*

- *A God that doesn't look at the numbers (ICP) because He is all about bringing glory to His name and drawing people to Him by using us and this accident as a tool to do just that.*
- *God working a miracle healing in John's brain and body.*
- *John now walking, talking, and loudly declaring the things God has done for him to all who will listen.*

Chapter 2

The Last Ride

April Keller

Almost every weekend John spent one day meticulously cleaning up his cars and motorcycle. Our two-year-old son, Caden, liked to help his daddy in this chore, so they had been outside cleaning and polishing the bike. Usually when they were through, John rode it around the block just to keep the battery charged. Caden loved to help work on the bike, but he did not like to hear it when John fired it up. That Sunday afternoon, John had toyed with the idea of going golfing, but since he had made the decision that it was time to sell his bike, he wanted to take advantage of the beautiful winter day and go for one more ride.

In many parts of the nation, a mid-February afternoon means a day that is cloud-covered, chilly with snow or perhaps rainy and wet. However, in South Texas, it means a gorgeous, sunny afternoon with no clouds in the sky and a perfect 89 degrees. John just could not resist any longer. He had heard about some bull riding going on in a neighboring community, and he wanted to check it out to see if it was something Caden would enjoy. John took off down the street, and just as I could no longer hear the engine roaring, the boys were down for a nap, and I was going to relax for a little while.

Fifteen minutes after John left the house on his bike, my phone rang. I saw that it was John's phone calling and wondered what he had forgotten. As I said, "Hello," I realized it was not John's voice on the phone. The person on the other end, whom I later met, asked if I was John's wife and then proceeded to tell me John had been in an accident. *An accident*, I am thinking, *John Keller...Mr. Invincible...no way!* The stranger said John was hurt and was going to the hospital in an ambulance. I asked which hospital and then put in a call to John's parents. The man had tried to call them but couldn't get through. All along I am thinking, *John probably just got a little bump, and they make everyone ride in an ambulance when there has been an accident...John is FINE!* Boy was I wrong!

I immediately started making arrangements for someone to come and take care of the boys. I scrambled around the house and was calling my mom at the same time because I had both boys asleep and, obviously, could not take them to the hospital. By the time my mom and step-dad arrived, I had pumped milk for the baby, not knowing when I was coming home, threw some clothes on and ran out of the house.

On my drive to the hospital, I called my dad and told him what had happened. I said, "I am not sure how bad it is, but it doesn't sound that bad." My dad said they were already packing to come. I told him to wait until I could find out how bad it was, but, apparently, he had talked to James and knew more than I did at that point in time. I made another phone call to John's best friend, Robert, and told him the same thing, "I am not sure how bad it is, but I will get back with you." I was still thinking: *John is fine!*

When I arrived at the hospital shortly thereafter and found Jan and James outside pacing and praying, I knew this was not a good sign. James was on the phone, and a few other friends were waiting. John had been taken into a trauma treatment room to be examined. I overheard James say that they had put John into an induced coma. This is when I suddenly realized how serious John's injuries were, and now I was really scared. At this point, I still did not know how bad it was about to become. After some more huddled praying outside, the doctor called in the family. James and I went in to see John.

John laid on the emergency room table - this huge guy, my husband, strong, tall and handsome; only now he was in an induced coma with blood coming out of every orifice of his face. He was covered with a sheet up to his neck so I couldn't see any bodily injury besides what was already evident. In walked a petite man, who turned out to be the neurosurgeon. I don't quite recall what all he said except that he felt John needed to be operated on immediately to control the bleeding in his head. I don't remember how dismal he was predicting the surgery to be. I just remember saying, "Oh no, John is going to be fine. He is a strong guy, and my husband will be just fine."

To see John lying there, with his feet hanging off the table and his body width barely fitting on the table to begin with, and then this doctor telling me that the outcome might not be good was too much for me to comprehend. How could I accept this from someone who didn't know my John and how strong he was? Obviously, I did not understand everything about the severity of the injuries, but I just knew John could make it, and he would not be happy barely making it with any disabilities. If he wasn't back to being old John, then he wouldn't want to be here.

The doctors were actually amazed that John had not sustained far worse injuries considering the way he was hit. Since John loved working out, he was very athletic. So, when he hit the pavement after being thrown 150 feet into the air, his muscles secured all of his limbs keeping them from injury. He had no broken arms or legs. Even though John was not wearing a helmet, Jan thanked God for an answer to her early morning prayer. John's head was covered by the helmet of salvation. Yes, there was serious injury but he was alive.

The first report was not good. The doctor was not optimistic about any kind of a recovery, let alone a full one. There was no time to life flight John anywhere because he was bleeding so badly. Also, John's pelvis was broken in three places and needed to be addressed immediately. The doctor went on to explain John had fractured his skull, and now this was complicated by the swelling of his brain

The orthopedic surgeon came in just about that time. It was a relief to see Dr. Fulp walk through the door. My mom, who is a nurse, had worked for him just a year or so ago. She always said he was the best at what he did, and she would have him work on her grandkids if needed. So, I knew we were in good hands with him. We agreed that both the neurosurgeon and orthopedic surgeon should operate one right after the other. Apparently, the pelvic damage that John had sustained could cause him to bleed to death because the area was so vascular. Therefore, it was necessary to operate at once. We were so grateful for Dr. Fulp's expertise. However, we were unaware of the long road ahead involving more life-threatening brain surgeries.

John was immediately taken into surgery. When the doctors and their assistants began assembling their team and entered into the operating room, one of John's friends, who made a living by selling titanium screws, saw John's name on the x-rays. He immediately came out to the waiting room to tell us that he would be in there praying during the surgery. And if that wasn't enough, it turned out that another one of the assistants, who would be monitoring John's spinal cord during the surgery, was the son of a close family friend. So again, the hand of the Lord was seen in His watchful care over John.

The neurosurgeon began the surgery and cut a piece of the skull out from the right side of the head to try to stop the bleeding. However, the family had been warned that with the swelling of the brain, it could cause more places to begin to bleed. John received fifteen units of blood during the surgery. When the neurosurgeon was done with his portion of the surgery, Dr. Fulp took over. He had previously explained that he would be using titanium goal posts to secure John's pelvis. Later, he told us it was a good thing that the people rendering aid at the accident site were able to keep John from trying to get up as this could have punctured any one of his vital internal organs. We were very grateful that God had His hand on John at the scene.

The "Good Samaritan" that watched over John at the scene and called me on John's cell phone had followed the ambulance to the hospital. When he met up with Jan and James later, he said, "I didn't know if anyone would be there yet, and I knew he would need prayer."

Time seemed to come to a crawl. No one really remembers how many hours went by before we finally heard from the doctor, but it seemed like forever. Dr. Fulp was the first to come out to report that he repaired John perfectly, and he should be great to walk in a few days! I thought, *What a relief!* Then the neurosurgeon came out shaking his head from side to side. He had a different story altogether. I don't remember all that the neurosurgeon said, but he thought he had stopped the bleeding and relayed to us that John had massive brain injuries. He said it was not uncommon for bleeding to pop up somewhere else in the brain, and he was right. Eventually it did.

We learned that ICP meant intracranial pressure, and we were educated very quickly about ICP numbers and began an intense watch over them. These numbers went up and down hourly as John lay in his induced coma. Several times the doctor or nurse came to check on John and turn his sedation medicine off. Then they watched his reaction by just giving him time or inflicting pain on him. They could tell how the brain was injured based on the arm movements he would make. When they pushed on his fingernail real hard, they were looking for an arm jerking back to protect oneself type of reaction. Instead they got this awful arms turning inward towards the body movement, which indicated there was pressure building up in John's brain. This was so hard to watch. At first we were excited to see his movement until we learned that the reaction they were getting was not a good one.

John was moved to the intensive care unit. The neurosurgeon did not give us much hope, if any. John wasn't getting any worse, but he wasn't getting any better. He was in tremendous pain, and his brain was still bleeding. Our journey to bring John back to wholeness had only just begun.

• • •

KEYS TO WALKING OUT A MIRACLE:

1. Stand firm in what God says He will do.
2. Guard your eyes and your heart from the trauma and pain that may come your way in tragic events.

Miracle Testimony

Stephen Sutton

I have known John since at least 1989. I grew up in McAllen, TX and went to McAllen High School while John went to Memorial High School. We were both active in sports and have been friends over the years. The Keller's are one of the most godly families I have ever met. They greet everyone with a smile and a joyful attitude and are constantly helping people. They never miss the opportunity to share what God has done in their lives and what He can do in yours.

On Sunday evening February 17, 2008 I had just finished consulting on a surgery with Dr. Fulp at McAllen Medical Center. After changing clothes and heading to church, the operating room at the hospital called. They had a motor vehicle accident involving a motorcycle, and Dr. Fulp was requesting me to provide instrumentation and implants for the surgery.

I hurried back to the hospital and changed into my scrubs, hair cover, and mask as fast as possible. When I entered Operating Room #1, Dr. Fulp was working on the patient, and the room was full of medical staff. I turned to the wall to begin looking at the x-rays and MRI to prepare a plan for the instrumentation. My back was to the patient when one of the nurses said, "This is one big white guy." Just then, I looked up at the top of the screen at the patient name

- J. KELLER. I couldn't think of any bigger white guy in the Valley with the name J. Keller than my friend, John. My heart sunk into my chest as I turned around to look at the patient. He was lying in a prone position (face down), and I had no way of knowing who this patient was without looking at his face.

Then I realized, if this was the John Keller I knew, his family would be in the waiting room praying. I immediately left the operating room, and as I walked out of the surgical suite, I could see through the glass into the waiting room. About 30-40 people were standing with hands joined, praying to the Lord. John's mother and sister came over to speak with me but didn't know until I took off my mask that it was me — a friend. A part of me wanted to break down and cry, but I had to be strong for this wonderful family. I told them I had no idea it was John in the operating room until I saw his name on the x-ray.

It was urgent that I quickly return to the operating room, but I promised to come out and give them up-to-the-minute information and to surround John with prayer throughout the surgery. I reassured them that the medical team was doing everything they could to give John the best care possible. However, inwardly I was reminded that this family was looking to the "One" who was truly in control — the Great Physician, Christ Jesus! They amazed me with their great faith and the fact they were going straight to the Lord in prayer.

We worked for a few hours on John in that operating room and then began to close up. As I prayed during the surgery, I knew John's life was hanging in the balance, and the most serious issue would be the Intercranial Pressure (ICP) that was being exerted on John's brain. As a father, I could only imagine the thoughts going through the minds and hearts of this special family. I knew John had a wonderful wife and two precious children at home. Dr. Fulp tried to give the family hope as he spoke with them after the surgery.

James told me from the first day that he believed God was going to raise John up and let him walk out of the hospital. No one knows God's timing, but I believe James walked in faith because eleven months after the accident, John started talking and walked out of the hospital at the end of January 2009.

I couldn't believe what I saw when I looked at a video of John doing therapy in Houston. Each day he seemed to get better. After John came home, I happened to be driving by the Keller's office and saw him walking up the stairs to the 2nd floor offices. I turned my car around to go back to see him. I ran up those steps, opened the door and stood in awe of God's healing power in the life of John Keller. I reached out to give John a hug, and he reached back to hug me. I couldn't believe this young man, who I thought might die or be paralyzed, was standing before me.

I am so thankful to have seen God's power work in the Keller's lives. I am challenged by their faith in the Lord, and I count it a blessing to have been part of this miracle. In this God has reminded me that He is sovereign, He is Holy, and He cares for His children.

Chapter 3

The Journey Begins

James Keller

Jan pulled into the driveway at my dad's house as I was trying to get my bike started to go join John. When she told me that John had been hit by a car on his bike, but they didn't think it was too bad, I kind of freaked out. We immediately headed for the hospital and were waiting at the emergency room when the ambulance arrived. As the ambulance doors opened, it was evident that John was hit hard. The EMS attendants said he was in tremendous pain and not cognizant of his injuries as he kept fighting to get off the gurney. He was extremely strong and had already pulled all the IVs out of his arm. I asked John to calm down while the doctors and paramedics were trying to help him. He was immediately sedated and taken in for assessment.

When April and I went into the treatment room to see John for the first time, he was completely chilled out. It was tough to see him like that. The doctor said, "We don't know how bad it is. We're going to have to check it out further, but we know he has a brain injury and his pelvis is broken in three places. We need to know if you want us to operate."

April and I agreed to have them operate right away both by the neuro-surgeon to address the brain swelling and bleeding and by the orthopedic surgeon to repair the broken pelvis. Then the doctor again said, "We don't know how this is going to turn out." But April replied, "No, you don't understand. My husband is a very strong man, and he's going to be just fine! My husband is going to be just fine!"

That key statement was exactly what came out at the Conference in January. When something hits you that you don't expect and it's bad, you have to begin to decree what you *want* to have happen. That decree then begins to change what is actually happening, even though it doesn't look like it has happened yet. She started it off and stood in faith when she said, "No, he's going to be just fine."

Word spread quickly through the community as family and friends flooded to the hospital. Some lived close by but others came from far away to be with us at the hospital to pray or to help with childcare for the small grandchildren. The emergency room became so overwhelmed with people coming in who were concerned for John that the hospital locked the emergency room doors. Everyone was ushered to a second-floor waiting room, which became a prayer, praise and worship sanctuary.

As the evening progressed and as friends and family gathered in the waiting room praying and worshipping God, two Scriptures came forth immediately. The first was II Kings 4:26 KJV, concerning the Shunammite woman.

Run now, I pray thee, to meet her, and say unto her, Is it well with thee? Is it well with thy husband? Is it well with the child? And she answered, "It is well."

I remembered immediately that the Scripture had been taught at the "Starting the Year Off Right" Conference just a few weeks earlier! It was amazing how it paralleled what was going on in our situation. The Shunammite woman was the mother of a son. In this case, Jan was the mother of the son. The son was playing in his father's yard when he got hurt with a head injury. John was at one of the family-owned stores that day (in his father's yard), just before he suffered a head injury. In the Bible, it was an accident. In John's case, it was an accident. It was not something that was planned by God, it was just an accident, and even though it was bad, the family knew that God could turn it for good.

The boy in II Kings died on his mother's lap. The mother took the boy and put him in the prophet's room and ran to the prophet. She didn't say anything to anyone, even her husband, except to declare, "It is well."

The Shunammite woman refused to accept second best, because she knew that only the prophet could do what was necessary to save her son. She put a demand on the prophet to come with her.

The Word of God says that children are a gift from God as it says in Psalm 127:3 NAS, *"Behold, children are a gift of the Lord, The fruit of the womb is a reward."*

One lesson I learned through all of this was that John was a gift, but the actual ownership of John belongs to God Almighty. God ordained John, God had a plan for John, and God wanted that plan to work. The beautiful thing about it is that God cares for and loves John even more than anyone of us could. We decided that instead of cursing God for this tragedy, we would bless God, no matter what we saw happening around us. John's name means "The Lord is gracious," and we clung to God's grace to take us through this unexpected event to an expected victory.

The second Scripture that came that night was Psalm 118:17 NKJV; "*I shall not die, but live, and declare the works of the Lord.*"

In my determination to hear from God, I look for every confirmation that I can possibly find. I soon realized that the number "seventeen" in the Bible means *victory*. John was hit on February 17th and he was admitted to room 26 of the ICU, which paralleled with the verse number 26 from II Kings 4:26. Thank God! He had ordained that John would live and not die! That was a tremendous confirmation but walking through it was a different story. We could not just take that Scripture and walk away. We had to take it and carry it and walk it out every day. That was the hard part, because that's what it means to walk by faith.

More and more family and friends arrived at the hospital. John and April's pastor came and prayed according to the Word of God that John's days are not finished on this earth. I, also, prayed that John's days are not finished and that he would be a finisher of his race here on earth because John's two boys need their dad to raise them to be fine Christian men.

Looking unto Jesus the author and finisher of our faith; who for the joy that was set before him endured the cross, despising the shame, and is set down at the right hand of the throne of God.

Hebrews 2:12 KJV

In the waiting room during the afternoon, I shared this with the group that had assembled there:

"Earlier in the day when they were assessing John, the news from the doctor was not good. He was not optimistic at all about any kind of a recovery. We were told that the best we could hope for was a vegetative state or a life in a wheelchair. We will not accept that. This afternoon, when April said the words, 'John is going to be fine, my husband will be just fine;' at that moment, that very statement changed the tone of everything. Just as the Shunammite woman said, 'It is well,' April set a level of faith in the atmosphere. This was the very action that was talked about at the January Conference about declaring and decreeing those things in your life that are out of control. It did not matter what it looked like, April declared, 'John is going to be just fine.' Jan then added 'We don't go by what we see; we go by what we know' and with that, the theme of this journey suddenly became very clear."

John's best friend all through high school, Robert Christian, is in the military. Upon hearing about John's accident from April, Robert went directly to his commander and told the commander that he needed to be with John. He arrived in McAllen that night.

Robert's first order of business was to organize and establish a Night Watch for John. Robert's mother is an intercessor, and he knew how important it would be to have someone there at night praying. Robert gathered up John's two brothers-in-law, Rex and Jon, along with John's brother Charles, and the four men stood watch over John at night. This was confirmation to the family as we knew about the importance of Night Watches in Scriptures. It was, also, another way God was showing us that He knew exactly where we were and what was happening. We couldn't fight this battle alone. We needed prayer and praise warriors to hold up our hands and help carry us through to victory.

None of us were ready for the journey this accident would take us on. The family went home at midnight to rest and get ready for the battle that we knew was ahead of us. As we left, the Night Watch began.

• • •

KEYS TO WALKING OUT A MIRACLE:
1. Begin to decree what you *want* to have happen, even though it doesn't look like it has happened yet.
2. Gather those around you who will stand in prayer and agreement for what you are declaring.
3. Establish prayer watches 24/7.
4. Look for every confirmation you can possibly find of God's love and promises on which to stand.

Miracle Testimony

Robert J. Christian

I've known John Keller since I was in the seventh grade, and he has been my best friend ever since. We played basketball together in high school and were pretty much inseparable till we left for different colleges. He was always a wonderful example for others in high school as a Christian young man known for not drinking, cursing, carousing, etc. Highly respected by his teachers and peers, I was proud to call him my friend.

After college and time in the Army, John and I "reconnected" and visited when my assignments would permit. It's been exciting to see the two of us; "grown up", married, kids coming along, etc. Our last major trip before the accident was when we went to Hawaii to be in my twin brother's wedding.

We've always encouraged each other through ups and downs. I remember when his son, Caden, was in the hospital for weeks due to an illness they couldn't figure out. I think that was the lowest I'd ever heard John's spirits. I remember sitting in the stands with him for a NASCAR race, and him showing me the hairs standing up on his arm from excitement.

The day of the accident, April called me saying John had been hit on his bike. As my wife and I sat there beginning to pray, April called back and said it was serious. I told Leilani, "I've got to go," and she agreed. I got to McAllen Medical Center that evening to find a waiting room full of people standing in a circle praying. I expected nothing less from the Keller family. John's parents were my "second parents" growing up and a huge influence on my life to this day.

The next couple of weeks were a blur; from McAllen to Houston and then my return home to Fort Bliss, El Paso, TX. It was a roller coaster of fear and faith, excitement and despair, and lessons from God daily. I found myself on highs of faith that I'd never experienced before and in pits of confusion and temptation to give up hope daily.

The two rocks through it all were Jan, his mother, and April, his wife. These women stood on faith in God's power and never wavered once, while the men needed constant reassurance from the Lord to hold fast and not give up.

Because of "Army stuff" - school, training, missions, etc. - it was almost a year-and-a-half after Houston before I'd see John again. During that time, I witnessed the miracles through the family blog, phone calls and emails. I remember the day April called and said, "John wants to talk to you!" He got on the phone and clear as a bell said, "Hey Rob, what's going on?" I was floored. Then last summer I arrived at the beach condo on South Padre Island and about fell over as John came walking out to greet my family. He gave me a big old hug, and I "really" grasped the fact that my friend was going to be O.K.

In the time since then, we call every few days or so; and week-by-week he tells me how his sight is improving, how God is speaking to him, and how glad he is to be a miracle! I can hear his thoughts and speech getting clearer and clearer, and every time we speak, he sounds "more" like John. The John I loved growing up, the John I related to as a young man, and the John who continues to inspire me to be a better Christian, husband, father, and son.

Chapter 4

Prayer and Praise
Set the Stage

Jan Keller

We were still somewhat in shock that Monday, February 18th, the day after the accident. The Intensive Care Unit was on the second floor of the hospital, and there were two separate waiting rooms just down the hall from the ICU entrance. The visiting hours for ICU were four times a day and only for fifteen minutes each time. Many families camped out in these waiting rooms all day and never left the hospital, waiting for their precious fifteen-minute visiting period. Fortunately, our family was granted favor and had access to and from John's room as often as we liked.

The larger waiting room in the corner became the staging ground of this vigil. Its location sat over the entrance to the hospital with four large windows facing out the front of the hospital, overlooking the front parking lot. The prayers that flowed out of that room spilled over onto everyone that passed through those doors beneath.

We were so thankful when the McGuire family, whom we have known for over thirty years, came from Houston to stand in prayer with us for John. They literally left in the middle of their Sunday night life-group meeting at their home to fly down and be with us. Not only did the life group begin to intercede and stand with us, their entire church, Fellowship Church of the Woodlands, continued to pray through this entire journey with John.

One of the McGuire's daughters, Heather, who is closest to John's age, is a registered nurse so we were encouraged because this meant she knew specifically how to pray for John's medical needs. Heather's sister, Stephanie, who has her own personal miracle child by the name of Jadyn, also knew how to help us pray. Jadyn was born 26-weeks premature, weighing less than two pounds. Both mother and daughter had multiple complications, and during their walk through this very difficult time, we stood in prayer with them. Today, Jadyn is a happy, healthy, very normal little girl and is a testimony to the power of prayer. We know how important it is in a walk like this to have people around us that know what to look for and then how to pray strategically. April's mother and our daughter Jené's in-laws are also registered nurses, so this encouraged us even more.

Many people stayed with our family the first night, but we could not believe how many continued to come to the hospital in the following days. Words of encouragement, dreams, visions, and Scriptures started pouring in from everywhere. People we had not spoken to or seen in years came forward to express their support and pray.

One of the first dreams that surfaced came from a man we had never met. Barney Sarver, the Fellowship of Christian Athletes Coordinator for the Rio Grande Valley, and his wife Cheri have been close family friends for many years. Our two families raised our kids together. Barney was actually headed to an FCA Conference on Sunday when he received the news about John and turned around to come back to be with us. On Monday, Barney learned that one of the FCA men at the Conference upon hearing of the accident the night before began praying for John. This man had never met John and had no knowledge of him other than what Barney had disclosed. The man told Barney that he had a vision of a tall, slender but very muscular young man, sharing about the victory of almost being killed in a motorcycle accident and declaring the works of the Lord to a congregation. We grabbed onto that vision and believed it was from the Lord.

Around 5:00 pm, it was decided that John needed to be taken back into surgery to have a filter put into his main artery. This was to safeguard against blood clots in his legs. If a clot came about, it would be captured by the filter thereby not allowing it to move into John's lungs, heart or brain. We began to pray against blood clots in the arms, because there was nothing that could be done to safeguard against that. When someone is immobilized in bed for a long time, as in this case, blood clots are serious potential problems. We just had to trust God that He would not allow any blood clots to form in John's arms.

John was kept heavily sedated in ICU, and a twenty-four-hour prayer watch was set up. The Night Watch came in late at night and left early in the morning. During the daytime numerous people came in and out to pray for John and the family. At any given time in the waiting room, you could hear songs being sung, the Word being confessed and people praying. Tears flowed as well as joy and laughter spilled out, but through it all, the praise for God never stopped. People reconnected with each other after having been apart, some even for years! It was almost like a Holy Ghost family reunion! It presented a brief glimpse of what heaven will be like once we are all there together!

People were sending emails and text messages letting the family know that they were praying. It was phenomenal! You could feel the complete and total support from the body of Christ, family, friends, employees, and the community — even the family's business competitors came and supported us. They were all standing with us in prayer and agreeing for John's healing — to live and not die.

James gave the instruction that the focus had to be 24/7 prayer. We were asking God to raise John up right out of that bed and heal him. When we were not seeing John jumping up out of that bed, we knew we could not let that affect us, our faith or our beliefs. God would do what He said He was going to do. We just had to be patient and wait on Him.

Then we started to notice something unusual occurring. Other people not associated with us began to come in and bring prayer requests for their own situations. This included visitors to the hospital who were there to see other patients, hospital employees on their lunch breaks or after their shift was done, and patient's families that came in to join us each day. We prayed and ministered to those people about our walk. We always tried to minister to those around us, as much, if not more, than we did to each other.

Walking through this time with John in ICU, the major focus was on the ICP numbers. Intracranial pressure (ICP) is the pressure in the *cranium* and in the *brain tissue* and *cerebrospinal fluid*. This pressure is exerted on the brain's intracranial blood circulation vessels. ICP is maintained in a tight normal range. One of the most damaging aspects of brain trauma and other conditions, directly correlated with poor outcome, is an elevated intracranial pressure. ICP is very likely to cause severe harm if it rises too high and is usually fatal if prolonged. An increase in pressure, most commonly due to head injury can create all kinds of problems.[1] The numbers had to stay around the 15-to-17 range and not go over 20. All of the time, we were just praying for the numbers to stay low.

It was early Tuesday morning, February 19th when James and I were awakened by a text message from the Night Watch. The text said that the doctor was going to have to start giving John some medicine because his brain had started to swell. As we began to pray, we looked at the clock and it was 3:14 am. So, we got out the Bible and looked up John 3:14 KJV: *"And as Moses lifted up the serpent in the wilderness, even so must the Son of man be lifted up."*

After reading the Scripture, I said, "God just showed us that the serpent lifted up on the pole in the wilderness is the sign today used for medicine." James and I agreed in prayer that this medicine would help lift John up, just like Jesus was lifted up.

Later, we found out the name of the medicine used to help John was called Mannitol. What was even more amazing was the definition of Mannitol. Wikipedia describes Mannitol as an *organic compound.* "This polyol is used as an osmotic diuretic agent and a weak renal vasodilator. It was originally isolated from the secretions of the flowering ash, called manna after their resemblance to the biblical food, and is also referred to as mannite and manna sugar."[2] John was receiving manna from heaven! Thank you, Lord!

About 7:00 am on Tuesday, Garrison, the five-month-old infant son of John's youngest sister, Jené and her husband Jon, woke up crying. Jené soothed him the best she could but determined everything to be fine, so, she began to intercede and pray for John. Garrison calmed down as she prayed. We later found out that this coincided with John's blood pressure spiking about that time. The blood pressure elevation helped the doctors determine that John was in pain, and they took measures to begin to administer morphine to ease it. I believe God will use little children to get our attention! Even to this day, if you ask Garrison who it was we prayed for that was in a motorcycle accident, he will tell you, "Uncle John."

Tuesday morning, February 19th, James and I went in with Dr. Fulp to see John. He looked so good. We began to talk to him and noticed there was some type of a control box there that beeped with an audible sound and a blinking indicator light. I told John that I knew he could hear us, and right then he started to flex his chest! I began to sing to him "Jesus… Jesus…" and the box started beeping faster in response! Then he flexed his chest again! I told John we were there, and we just wanted him to rest and heal. While we were in with John, I learned that there was a video camera feedback to the nurse's station, where a nurse is always watching the patients. I thought, *Praise God, we have guardian angels watching over him all of the time!*

The neurosurgeon came and reported that he saw two good things through the night. John's ICP numbers were good and the blood work was good. This meant it was time to start decreasing the sedation medicine to see if he would wake up.

Robert, John's best friend and one of the Night Watchmen, noticed that as he talked to him, John would begin to move around. Then, Robert began to sing to John over and over, "*Strength will rise as we wait upon the Lord, we will wait upon the Lord, we will wait upon the Lord.*" I, also, noticed that John moved around as I talked to him. This let me know that John was hearing us.

Back in the waiting room later in the day, everyone was in prayer and did not hear a young woman come in and approach the vending machine. One of the women in the Keller group noticed her and saw that she was visibly burdened. She approached the woman and asked if she could pray for her. The woman said she got off the elevator on the wrong floor and was not even thirsty but was drawn to the waiting room. She said that her mother and father were not saved, and she wanted the Lord to save them. James had just rejoined the group and everyone prayed for her. This is just another example of how by pouring into the people that were there – whether they were there for John or not - God poured back into our family. God continually let us know He was watching over all of us.

The rest of the evening on Tuesday was spent just as the previous two evenings had been – with the sounds of praise and prayers! God's people heard the call and responded! At 10:00 p.m., the Night Watch took over.

• • •

James Keller

Bright and early Wednesday morning, February 20th, found me on my knees beside John's bed. I told God I needed a sign for good. Just then, as if on cue, one of the nurses stuck her head in the door and asked if James Keller was in the room. I told her I was James Keller, and she said I had a phone call at the desk. I couldn't figure out who would be calling me at the nurse's desk, but I went to take the call.

I picked up the phone and said, "This is James Keller," and it was Dr. Fulp's voice on the other end. All he said was, "Hey, I heard Jesus walked into John's room last night." That was all I needed to hear! Praise God! Jesus was in the room last night with John! How much more could I ask for? The Word of the Lord came forth again:

> *Jesus said to her, "Did I not say to you that if you would believe you would see the glory of God?*
>
> John 11:40 NKJV

Confirmations continued to come all day long that God knew exactly what was going on, where the family was and that He was with us. Later in the morning, Jan received an encouraging call saying that the entire student population of Covenant Christian Academy (a local private Christian school) went outside to pray for John in the pavilion. We later learned that the school continued to pray for John each and every day through this journey.

Train a child in the way he should go, and when he is old he will not turn from it.

Proverbs 22:6 NIV

Jan was sitting in the waiting room visiting with people who had come to pray and noticed she had a missed call on her cell phone. She momentarily lost her breath when she saw that it was a call from John's cell phone. She realized quickly that it had to be either Charles (John's brother) or Robert (John's friend) that was calling from his phone, but she whispered to John's spirit, "John, I am sorry I missed your call, but I know what you are saying. You are coming home!"

Another CT scan revealed more bleeding in John's head. He would now require a third surgery to try to stop the bleeding. Everyone was back to the task at hand, praying for John, the neurosurgeon, the nurses, the equipment and for God's perfect healing. Jennifer, John's older sister, said, "God is what He says He is and God will do what He says He will do." The rest was left up to God.

After the surgery was over, the neurosurgeon came down the hall, and said that even though he was able to get the bleeding to stop, he believed the pressure had done damage to John's brain. We continued to pray, "John has the mind of Christ and he is covered by the blood of Jesus and no weapon formed against him shall prosper."

Shortly thereafter, Dr. Fulp, the orthopedic surgeon, came to me and said he wanted me to go in and pray with him over John and his "little bump on the head" as he called it.

Dr. Fulp is quite a character. He completely devotes himself to his patients often staying at the hospital for days at a time, "forgetting" to go home. Sometimes, his wife has to come looking for him to bring clean clothes because he has not been home. He is a tall man of average build and describes himself as a "simple redneck." It was not uncommon to see him dressed in scrubs with his cowboy boots on. He has an infectious smile, one that stretches from ear to ear, and a compassionate heart. You cannot help but be drawn to this man and then laugh the entire time you are with him. He has a gift of joy and kindness comes from his mouth all of the time. We came to revere him as a guardian angel for John.

Dr. Fulp and I went into John's room and knelt beside the bed. Dr. Fulp told the Lord that he wanted to see a miracle for John. With everyone exhausted emotionally, spiritually and physically, the Night Watch took over at 10:00 p.m.

When the family arrived at ICU early on Thursday morning, February 21st, the Night Watchmen were sent home to sleep. The word came forth that this would be a "grace and favor" day. God spoke through a friend the words, "anticipatory medicine," and we had seen the Lord do that over and over through the past few days. When Jan went back to the room to watch and pray over John, the ICP numbers began to escalate. She asked the Lord what to do. The latest CT scan had been ordered and done, but it had not been read yet. About that time, the supervisor for the ICU came in, hooked up with her faith and said, "John will see his daughter get married." Jan told her that he only had two sons, and the supervisor said that God had shown her John would see his daughter get married. Jan said, "AMEN! I receive that prophecy!"

By 10:00 am, John had not had any more Mannitol. He had been breathing by himself this entire time, and the ventilator was only working at 30%. However, the ICP numbers were still increasing little by little. Jan once again gave thanks to Jesus for the helmet of salvation on John's head. As the day went on and the numbers continued to increase, the neurosurgeon came and said, "John is hanging on by a thread." Jan thought that it was time to pray for his attitude because she felt like it needed an "adjustment." She immediately rebuked his statement, and said, "We declare that we are not hanging on by a thread, but by a three strand cord – the Father, Son and Holy Spirit."

> *And if one prevail against him, two shall withstand him; and a threefold cord is not quickly broken.*
>
> Ecclesiastes 4:12 KJV

Every time the number increased, Jan began to declare the number null and void in the medical sense and began declaring their biblical value. She said, "15 means *rest*…17 means *victory*…19 means *faith*."

• • •

April Keller

I felt differently about the ICP numbers. I know that most people were looking at the numbers and going by them, but I never felt like being at a specific number meant life or death. I know others wanted to pray them down, but I felt like it was John's whole picture that needed to be looked at, and a number couldn't tell us everything about John's state of being or his recovery.

I was so grateful for family and friends at this point in time. Without them I could not have juggled our life during these difficult, critical days. I stayed at the hospital most of the day and late into the night. While at the hospital, I had to pump milk every 2-3 hours for our newest son, Dalton, who was just 2 months old. I tried to run home to see our boys at least a few hours a day. Thankfully, my dad and step-mom were retired and had come to help out with the kids. They were amazing and very generous with their time during those first days and in the months to follow. Luckily, the kids didn't have a clue what was going on, but they started to recognize things weren't the same.

Little did I know how our lives were about to be turned upside down for the next year. Being a stay-at-home mom was my life. I loved it and still love it, but things were about to change, and no longer could I focus on our kids full time.

We started looking at our options while being by John's side. As every day got harder and the scenario got scarier, more people kept flooding in the waiting room to pray for us and be with us. I was being asked to make decisions that I didn't think I could make.

When I told that to Jan, she said, "I can't make those decisions by my-self either, so we will be like Ruth and Naomi. Wherever you will go, I will go, and whatever you do, I will do." And that is what we did in the months ahead!

• • •

KEYS TO WALKING OUT A MIRACLE:

1. Gather people around you that know what to look for and how to pray strategically for your situation.
2. Be patient and wait on the Lord.
3. Turn negative reports into positive declarations based on what the Lord's Word says.
4. Keep prayer and praise going forth continually.
5. Link arms with faithful partners when making difficult decisions.

Miracle Testimony

Jené Keller Byrom

I am John's younger sister, and I have the blessing of working with John every day in our family business. He has always been a very disciplined and driven person, working out before coming to work and being the first one in the office each day. We often found each other at the office on Sunday afternoon getting work done before Monday started a new week.

On Sunday, February 17*th* my husband, Jon, our son, Garrison, and I were visiting my cousin in Dallas. Unexpectedly, I received a phone call from Maria, who works with John, alerting me that something was very wrong. I then called my dad, and he told me John had been in a bad motorcycle accident, and he and my mom were waiting for the ambulance to arrive at the hospital. At that same time, I had a text message from April saying, "Please pray for John. He has been in a motorcycle accident, and we don't know how bad it is."

Once the ambulance arrived, my dad called and said I needed to pray for John to live and not die because he hit his head and it didn't look good. Our return flight from Dallas was scheduled that afternoon, so we were heading to the airport. It was scary to be so far away and then to board a plane without any communication for over an hour. My oldest brother, Charles, lives in Dallas, *and he got on the same flight to McAllen with us. When we landed, we drove directly to McAllen Medical Center. As I walked into the waiting room, I was so glad to see my family and then to see how many people were there praying and believing with us for John.*

I didn't really comprehend how serious this was until I saw John in ICU in a coma. That was so hard, but my dad told me I had to have faith to walk through this, and I couldn't give up. We needed to fight for John since he couldn't fight for himself. I hated to see him so badly hurt. But I, also, knew John was a fighter; and with God on his side, he could make it because he had never quit on anything.

The first few weeks I learned that we don't go by what we see but by what we believe. I am so thankful to my parents for teaching us that we walk by faith not by sight, and never once did anyone in our family think that God couldn't heal John and make him completely whole. I prayed certain Scriptures every night before I went to sleep and declared them over my brother. My baby was five months old, and when he would wake up in the middle of the night screaming, I knew it was God waking me up to pray. So, Garrison and I would pray for John. Garrison is now two years old, and he will tell you that Uncle John was in a motorcycle accident and hit his head, but he is all better. Just the other day, I was thanking God again for healing my brother, and Garrison said, "He's all better, Mom!" Then he clapped his hands and said, "YEAH!"

I held onto a vision someone shared about a tall man being involved in a motorcycle accident and six months later being totally healed. When six months came and John wasn't to that place yet, I remember asking God why but then realized God's timing always is perfect. I began standing on

Habakkuk 2:3: "For the revelation awaits an appointed time; it speaks of the end and will not prove false. Though it linger, wait for it; it will certainly come and will not delay." I knew God could do the impossible, and I declared over John that he would be made whole and complete and be better than he was before.

Just a few days after his accident, I had a dream of John sitting across from me at my parents' dining room table. He was talking to me, and he looked just like he did before the accident. In the dream our family was telling him everything that had happened, because he didn't remember anything about his accident. I am blessed to tell you that my dream has come true just like I saw it. John doesn't remember anything from the day he got hit or the eleven months thereafter. I know this road hasn't been an easy one for anyone, but God is faithful and He did what He said He would do. John is truly a miracle, and I am so blessed by what God has done in his life. I am thankful to the Lord and for all that prayed and agreed with us for John's complete healing.

Going through this with my family, I was amazed to see how my mom and dad didn't get consumed with only John's recovery but ministered to those around them as well. When John was in ICU at McAllen Medical, we had church in the waiting room. If there were other people in the waiting room with us, we prayed for their situation. In Houston when we went there on the weekends to see John, my mom knew all about the other patients and what their story was and how we needed to pray for them. It was a blessing to see my parents touch the lives of others in the midst of what our family was going through.

Chapter 5

Crisis Demands Action

James Keller

Could there possibly be any crisis that demanded action more than this one? Webster's Dictionary defines "action" as an act that one consciously wills and that may be characterized by physical or mental activity; a crisis that demands action instead of debate.1 Since all the family could do was pray and wait, we continued to minister to and pray for the people that came to the waiting room. Calls flooded in expressing love and support. Family and friends had been there for John 24-hours-a-day since the accident happened, and we were so blessed to have their involvement.

John's ICP numbers had been steadily elevating for the last 24 hours, which indicated that pressure was building in his head. By around noon on Friday, February 22th his ICP reached a very high level. It was determined more surgery would have to be done to remove pools of blood that were putting pressure on the brainstem. The Word that time came forth in prayer was:

> *Then I passed by and saw you kicking about in your blood, and*
> *as you lay there in your blood I said to you, "Live!*
>
> Ezekiel 16:6 NIV

The number "16" is the number for *love* in the Bible with "six" being the number for *man*. We interpreted that as God's love for John, the man.

Everyone began to pray and command the bleeding to stop and release the Spirit that abides in John to do the healing in John's body. As he was taken into surgery for the fourth time in five days to clean up bleeds and pressure on the brain stem, I suddenly felt angry with God. I will never forget how I struggled that day. I became so upset that I had to go out of the hospital and call my good friend, Chuck Pierce. Chuck is President of Glory of Zion International Ministries in Denton, Texas and has been a treasured personal friend for 30 years. I told him where I was in the middle of all of this and really fighting anger with God. I shared from my heart how I felt that if John died, God would have been a failure, my faith would have been a failure and my belief in the Word of God would have been a failure.

Needless to say, Chuck got me straightened out pretty quickly. He said, "James, if John dies, it's not going to hurt God's reputation." That word set me free! I realized that God is God, and I had given my life to God and would love God no matter what! I went back into the hospital and headed to the Chapel with Jan. Some very special men were already there praying. It was such a God moment! I gave John over to God on the altar, and I said, "God…he's Your son and if You take him home, then I am going to love You and serve You. And if You leave him here, I am going to love You and serve You." After I finished praying that soul-wrenching prayer from my heart — perhaps the toughest prayer I have ever prayed — God spoke to my heart and said, "James, I didn't take Isaac, and I am not going to take John." From that point forward, I found myself operating as Abraham did:

Then they came to the place of which God had told him. And Abraham built an altar there and placed the wood in order; and he bound Isaac his son and laid him on the altar, upon the wood. And Abraham stretched out his hand and took the knife to slay his son. But the Angel of the LORD called to him from heaven and said, "Abraham, Abraham!" So he said, "Here I am." And He said, "Do not lay your hand on the lad, or do anything to him; for now I know that you fear God, since you have not withheld your son, your only son, from Me."

Genesis 22: 9-12 NKJV

Just a few seconds later, the Lord spoke to me again in my heart and said, "The bleeding has stopped." Hallelujah! The bleeding has stopped!

Right at that moment, a woman came in and sat down in the prayer chapel. She was very upset and we asked if we could pray for her and she said, "Yes." She explained that she was having a real hard time with her family. Nobody was ill, but they were having a relationship problem. We began to pray for her, and the Lord gave us some specific Scriptures to pray over her. As we did, the spirit of fear broke off of her and peace and love came over her. It was a wonderful experience.

Jan and I went back upstairs to the second floor and we were met by a hospital employee who said the doctor wanted us escorted to a private room. We said, "No thank you, we will stay with our people." We continued to wait for the doctor to come and tell us what was happening because John was still in surgery. Within an hour, the neurosurgeon came and told us the two-hour surgery was successful. He said they had to remove some tissue from the brain, but the bleeding in John's head had stopped! Hallelujah! We rejoiced because that confirmed what the Lord had already told me.

Another thing I learned at this time was about the ICP numbers. When we try to figure out *how* God is going to heal a son or daughter or do a miracle in our own life, that's when we get messed up. In our walk, when the ICP numbers went up, we felt like our prayers were not being answered or that we were not praying properly. When they went down, we felt like we were having victory and that we were so-to-speak, "getting the job done."

My sister-in-law, who is a powerful prayer warrior, came to me and shared that the Lord said, "We just don't get it!" At that point, I was confused and a little angered, but I knew this was a serious message from the Lord. God spoke to me that night and said, "You are going to have to go in there and confess outright that the numbers are not what it's all about."

Earlier April shared how she felt about the ICP numbers not being the answer, but rather it was more important to focus on the total picture of John's situation. She wasn't sure the numbers could come down right at that point. To some that may have seemed like a lack of faith, but I believe she had caught a glimpse of what God spoke to me. It wasn't about the numbers! She knew healing was a process and John would be just fine!

About 6:00 p.m. each evening, we gathered together in the waiting room to talk, sing, preach, and or just brag on God. So, I went into the waiting room during our prayer meeting and confessed to them that I was praying for results, and if the results didn't go the way I thought they should, our prayers were not working. I then explained what God had shown me that it was not about the results we saw with our physical eyes. It was about Him and what He wanted to do and about us standing on the Word. God said it doesn't matter if mistakes are made; it doesn't matter if we or the medical team don't know what to do; it doesn't matter how we have gotten to where we are; what matters is that God is going to make everything right. I laid all that down, confessed it as sin and asked everyone to please forgive me. Our God was going to do what He said He was going to do, and it didn't matter what the numbers were.

As if God was sending a direct telegram straight to us, the next beautiful confirmation from God walked in the door of the ICU waiting room right then. We were having our prayer meeting and praise and worship time. A woman came in and was very distraught and crying uncontrollably for her son. Her mother, who was the boy's grandmother, was with her. The mom had on a t-shirt that said "Tough as Nails" with a picture of the nails with which Jesus was crucified. The grandmother had on a t-shirt that said "Warrior" on it.

Jan asked what happened, and they explained that the boy had been stabbed in the heart in a fight. The boy had yelled at a man that was stabbing a girl, and then the man turned on the boy and stabbed him right in the heart for trying to interfere. The mother told us her son was 18 years old and was from one of the local high schools.

I was listening in on the conversation and said, "My goodness, we are about to pray for our son — and briefly told her about John's story. Can we pray for your son, too?"

She said, "Yes, of course, please do."

So, we asked her and the grandmother to join our prayer circle, and we would agree together for her son's healing. I asked her, "What is your son's name?"

She replied, "His name is Isaac."

Looking back I can't believe I missed it, but I didn't pick up on the name, "Isaac." The same name as Abraham's son, in Genesis, Chapter 22. None of that fit for me right at that moment. We went on and prayed for Isaac. We agreed together in faith that he would live and not die; we declared healing over him, and that everything was working for his good - all the doctors, all the nurses, everyone involved in his case - and that Isaac was going to be just fine!

We found out later Isaac remained in the ICU for only two more days and was then admitted to a private room. Isaac's mother sought us out to tell us that a nurse had gone into his room, looked at him and said, "Rejoice, God has a plan for you! You should have died when you were stabbed in the heart, but, obviously, God has a plan for you, Isaac."

This confirmed for us that God is always faithful. Even in the middle of the worst situation you can be in, God is still standing right there. He never leaves us and He never forsakes us. God didn't take our John, and He didn't take this mother's Isaac either.

• • •

KEYS TO WALKING OUT A MIRACLE:

1. Seek godly counsel when you are struggling or feel like you're at the end of your rope.
2. Repent of unbelief when the going gets tough.
3. Release your burden to the Lord and let Him carry it.
4. Choose to continue to serve the Lord regardless of the outcome of your circumstances.
5. Gather around and pray for others who are hurting or needing a miracle as well.

Miracle Testimony

Patti Kohrt Munoz

I have known the Keller family since John was 10. I watched him grow up, graduate high school and college, get married and have children of his own. It was no surprise to me that immediately after word of the accident began to circulate, so many people flocked to the hospital to pray and support this family. We were in Best Buy, less than a half mile from the hospital, when the call came in, and we immediately left to go and pray. We didn't know how bad it was, but we wanted to be there for this family that had always been there for us.

Jan is a true Proverbs 31 woman and the rock of this family. I knew when she stood before us as a group, and said, "We don't go by what we see, we go by what we know" that this was so serious she would not even repeat the doctor's report in words. Life pretty much stopped for everyone that was connected with this family. Every waking moment was consumed with attending to the family and praying.

On Monday night February 18th, my husband, John, and I had just returned from the hospital. Everyone was exhausted and my body had finally given out. We prayed once more before laying down to sleep, and I asked God to help me understand how He saw this situation.

I finally allowed myself to sleep, and I had a "God" encounter that would forever change my life and impress upon me the need for intercessory prayer. It was actually early Tuesday morning, and I had been asleep for about three hours. I woke up to what I can only describe as a choir - but not a human-voice choir - they were angelic voices. The only words being sung were, "John Keller" over and over, but with pitches, harmonies and melodies like I have never heard before. They blended perfectly, and it was not a sorrowful song – it was one of rejoicing! As they sang, I could "hear" colors in their voices - the concept of "hearing colors" is totally foreign to me now, but, at the time, I completely understood it. I woke my husband up, but he did not hear anything. I looked at the clock and it was 3:14 am.

When I got to the hospital the next morning, I sought out Jan and James and told them what I had heard. The word came forth that God knew exactly where they were and that everything was in control because the angels were singing and proclaiming John's name! God honored my request and showed me how He saw the situation - He was rejoicing over John's life. I knew then, that given enough time, John would make a recovery. It was just a matter of time and prayer for wisdom.

It wasn't until I started gathering materials for this manuscript that I learned Jan and James had been awakened by the Night Watchmen at 3:14 am, saying that the doctor wanted to administer a medication to John because his brain had started to swell. We took it as confirmation that allowing the medication to be administered was a good thing. You'll read in the book about the medication being - Manna from heaven!

After realizing what God had showed me during the night, I never really stressed out over or questioned John's recovery. I just "stayed in my place," stood my ground, prayed as the family prayed and agreed with them on everything they believed for John's healing and recovery. Not too long ago, I told John Keller about that night, hearing the angels singing his name and rejoicing over his life. He began to weep and thanked God for healing him. He truly is a modern-day miracle.

Chapter 6

Seize Your Window of Opportunity

April Keller

The wee hours of early Saturday morning, February 23rd began with seeing John stabilized finally. The emergency room doctor had made it a habit of checking on the Night Watchmen each night to see if they were comfortable or in need of anything. When they saw him as they were leaving that morning, the doctor commented that Friday night in the emergency room was reminiscent of the war zone in Iraq. Isaac was only one of nine knifings that occurred Friday night. He told the Night Watchmen that John's ICP was at 19, which was a little elevated but stable. The Night Watchmen agreed that they were in a war zone as well and had prayed for the winds of change to come upon John and the family.

Jan had spent several hours with the Lord in the early morning. A word came to her through her good friend, Heather McGuire-Carr, who said she had a vision of a green sheet hanging on James' office wall behind his desk chair, with a word from the Lord written on it. The word said "THIS IS YOUR TIME TO MOVE FORWARD AND NOT TO TARRY. YOU HAVE A WINDOW OF OPPORTUNITY TO SEIZE AT THE MOMENT."

About that time, Jan looked up and saw the neurosurgeon coming down the hall, and he was smiling! She said, "Joy came all over me and I said to him, 'Amen! We have a good report!'"

The doctor said, "For the first time, we have a good report!"

Jan said, "Praise the Lord!" She started proclaiming the goodness of God shouting and saying, "You have declared Your Word over my son - he will stand and declare the works of the Lord!"

Later in the day, the neurosurgeon met with Jan, James and me in John's room. He showed us that John was off all sedation, but there was no response from him. John had now slipped into a real coma. The neurosurgeon pinched John on his neck, and he did not respond. He did the same on the other side of John's neck, and there was still no response. He used a flashlight in John's eyes to check the dilation of the pupils, and they did not move. He looked at us and said, "We have done everything we can do; now we will just have to wait."

James, Jan and I talked amongst ourselves and felt like we needed to begin to move toward the window of opportunity and go forward. I think we all knew the Valley (as local residents refer to the Rio Grande Valley) was not the place in which to bring John back to perfect health, so we started looking at our options. We were told Houston was the place to be and that was the direction in which we started heading. People were making calls, finding beds, finding a doctor, and looking for an air ambulance. It was amazing how it all worked out in God's perfect timing.

"Confirmation came in a unique way – and a huge way," recalled Jan. "Two different people, working independently of each other and unbeknownst to each other at the time, made contacts with the same doctor's office. First Heather made contact with the doctor in Houston that would agree to take John as a patient at The Methodist Hospital and then April's mother, wound up talking to the very same doctor's office! What a big God we serve!"

As the family was in the waiting room, talking amongst ourselves, a man from the local Methodist Church came in and said he was a visitor to ICU. His shirt had the logo on it for the Methodist Church, and the family took that as confirmation that it was time to move forward and begin looking at The Methodist Hospital in Houston, Texas.

Now that contact had been made with a doctor at The Methodist Hospital, James made a call on Sunday morning, February 24th and spoke directly to the neurosurgeon at the Neurosurgery ICU. He had looked at John's CT scans that had previously been sent to him. James asked him very simply, "Are you familiar with John?"

He said, "Yes."

James said, "I've never met you and I don't know how else to say this, so I am just going to simply ask you, do you think you could help John?"

He said, "Yes, I do."

James said, "Will you take John as a patient?"

He replied, "Yes, I will." He went on to explain that he would take John just as soon as there was a bed available, but, at the moment, every bed at The Methodist Hospital was full.

James said "Okay, praise God, as soon as you have a bed, we will transfer John to Houston."

Everyone had prayed and believed that God would show us what He wanted us to do. The doctors at McAllen ICU were saying it would be too risky to move John right now, and I told Jan I just couldn't take the responsibility to make that decision. She said, "Neither can I, so we'll just let God do it."

Jan added, "We had, also, been told that we could sign John out ourselves and 'take this window of opportunity.' What a confirmation! Those were the exact words that were seen on the sheet in Heather's vision. We had been praying that God would give us a 'window of opportunity,' but sometimes He has to speak loudly, so we will hear. I always prayed that I would have ears to hear, so I am always listening."

One of the ICU employees was in John's room with Jan and this woman was a believer. She asked Jan if she had a Scripture she was claiming. Jan replied, "Yes, I do: *'Ask, and it will be given to you; seek, and you will find; knock, and it will be opened to you,'* in Matthew 7:7 NKJV"

Later Sunday morning, James called and told me we were going to move John to Houston. I sprang into action and called my mother who is a registered nurse and has experience in the medical field. I thought James meant that we were making the move right then on Sunday, so we started packing bags and getting things lined up to leave right away.

Mom and I called James about the timing of the move. We did not want to hurt his feelings, but we had concerns that moving on Sunday was really not a good idea, because there would only be skeleton crews available for air ambulance services and hospital staffing. James clarified the miscommunication and explained that we weren't making the move on Sunday, as we had to wait for a bed to open up. He said it would be Monday or Tuesday or whenever God opened the door. We were in a waiting mode.

On Monday, February 25th, John was still heavily sedated and completely non-responsive. He was just lying there, in limbo, actually. It was a day of rest, healing and prayer. The waiting room was busy with activity all day long, people in and out, praying for and caring for the family and each other. Many opportunities to minister to outside people came along that day, and each and every one was embraced with open arms.

Jan woke up at 2:00 am early Tuesday morning, February 26th. When James asked what she was doing, she told him, "God told me to go to the hospital and get John ready. He is going to go to Houston today," and with that, she left for the hospital. James responded, "Praise God!" Jan faithfully and obediently went to the hospital and started cleaning out John's room and getting him ready for the transfer. At 9:00 am, the McAllen hospital called to say the Houston hospital had a bed ready for John Keller!

No sooner did the news about the bed availability make the rounds when fifteen minutes later, my cell phone rang. It was a call from the air ambulance company that they had a cancellation and could take us today - God's timing for sure!

I rushed home to pack bags. My dad and step-mom were going to take care of Caden and bring him to Houston later to be with me. Since I was nursing two-month-old Dalton, he would travel with me to Houston, which meant packing all the baby paraphernalia. It all happened so quick that it really didn't sink in that I was leaving my normal life, our home, my sweet dog Aggie, and our son to head to Houston for who knew how long. I didn't return home to McAllen for three months.

After I had packed and made arrangements for everyone, I headed to the hospital to wait for the ambulance to take John to the airport. We all followed the ambulance to the airport and watched and prayed for God's protection and grace as they squeezed John into a tiny, twin-engine plane, while he was in critical condition with massive brain injuries.

Thinking back on that day, putting John in someone else's hands and not being with him was very difficult for me. God had to be in control, because we sure didn't know what the pressure would do to his injuries, let alone the stress of traveling. Thankfully, my mom, a registered nurse, said she would fly with him so if they needed any help, she could assist. I think we all felt a little relief knowing John was not alone.

As John was in the air, we headed for Harlingen to board our flight to Houston. Once we landed in Houston and began traveling to The Methodist Hospital, we got word that John had landed and was still doing ok. He made it to the ICU at The Methodist Hospital, and we arrived soon after. A new chapter was beginning in John's journey to recovery.

• • •

KEYS TO WALKING OUT A MIRACLE:

1 Proclaim the goodness of God and declare His Word over your situation.
2. Look for and seize opportunities to shift into a new place as the Lord opens the door.
3. Fear not!
4. Find a specific Scripture to be your anchor in the storm.
5. Seek confirmation from the Lord and move forward.

Miracle Testimony

Stephanie McGuire Armstreet

B*eing a part of this journey with the Keller's has been full of pain and tears, sorrow and joy, but many times I was thrown into a bit of déjà-vu. Almost two years earlier, my husband and I were given the gift of life for our child to whom the world would have denied life. Suddenly, we were standing, watching and waiting to see the hand of God again move mightily in the midst of doctors, nurses and sometimes friends that did not understand what we knew – God's hand is still ever present. To stand and wait for God's perfect timing while longing for His action to be swift and complete is difficult. I watched my daughter, who was born at 1 lb. 9 oz., fight for life, while her brain was healing and still developing. I waited for her body to be able to breathe on its own, digest food properly and regulate her body temperature. Now I was waiting again for all these things to happen within John's body.*

Having watched this process happen before with my own daughter, I knew so much was possible when our Healer is involved. But that did not always make it easier to go through this with the Keller family. At times, I was desperate for John's healing to take place. We had received such a precious gift of which we were unworthy, and I needed to know that others were, also, recipients of such a gift of healing. For me, I often had an audible conversation with God begging for John's healing. During one such conversation, God told me He had already laid the foundation John would need for his healing; first to survive the accident and, secondly, He had already put people in their ordained positions around John and his family to restore him to health. That became my recurring prayer of gratitude, "Thank You for how You have already provided..." God provided for myself, Jeffery and Jadyn; and He provided for John and his entire family. He will continue to be the Provider for others.

Chapter 7

Authority Shifting

James Keller

Authority in the spiritual realm for John's healing was shifting from McAllen to the Houston area when the doctor in Houston accepted his case. I knew that we had to walk carefully and come into proper alignment as John was prepared to move to Houston. We waited and prayed.

We learned some key strategies that need to be followed when you are in a life and death battle:

1. When you have a Scripture from the Lord *stand* on that Word and *declare* that Promise over the situation.
2. Do whatever it takes to get the best care possible and never give up.
3. Weigh all the options and pray, pray, pray.
4. Move forward and don't be afraid to shift when the Lord opens the next door or window.

Faith works under authority. It's not a time to gripe and complain but to just keep praying and moving forward. Our prayer was Romans 8:28 that ALL things worked together for the good for John! When God was ready to move John, He put us in contact and alignment with the next doctor. We did not complain about or second guess the current doctor; we just knew that God was moving John to a new place. The Lord said that He would fix any mistakes, if any had been made, and not to worry or focus on any "what if's."

In the McAllen ICU, a girl that had had no brain activity for 18 days woke up while we were there! It was just incredible the level of faith, the number of prayers, the power of the anointing, and the glorious presence of God that was in that place. Many people walked into the ICU waiting room and were prayed for. Salvations came. Healing came. Relationships were restored. It was a miraculous time. God has had us minister to so many people through John's injury, and it continues even to this day. It is amazing to see how God will use you and how the anointing comes to help others when you are in the midst of your own crisis.

One of the main things to keep in mind when walking through something like this is that you cannot try to figure out how God is going to do something. If you try to do that, it's going to mess up how you pray.

We asked the Lord to reveal areas that we needed to know about *before* they became a problem to us or John, to uncover any hidden issues and to take any and all precautions so that John would live and not die. An example of this was the doctors putting in safety devices like filters to prevent any blood clots reaching his brain or lungs.

We made sure John was hydrated to keep all levels balanced in his organs and blood. We read the Word of God to him, played Christian music in his room and stayed by his side. We talked to him and constantly moved his arms, legs, hands and feet.

Many times, it might seem a lot easier to just agree with the diagnosis and stop working so hard, but we learned that you cannot do that. Jan and April and the rest of the family never quit on John and never quit on God. John never gave up and tried every day to do his best. Because we never gave up, no one at any of the hospitals or rehab center or nursing home ever quit either — not one doctor, not one nurse, not one therapist, not one technician. You just cannot accept what you are seeing in the physical or allow weariness to make you give up!

With moving John to Houston, the question arose of how to keep the people at home informed so they would know what to pray for while John was there. The answer was simple. John's sisters, Jennifer and Jené, created a blog that would keep everyone up to date and completely informed around the clock.

On Sunday, February 24, 2008, the first blog entry was made:

February 24, 2008:

John Keller was in a motorcycle accident on February 17th at 1:30pm. He was hit by a car pulling out of a shopping center in north McAllen. He was rushed to the hospital because he had sustained a serious head injury and a broken pelvis. John had both brain surgery to remove a blood clot and pelvic surgery to fix three fractures in his pelvis. They put him in an induced coma to reduce the swelling to his brain. Please pray for John, all of the medical staff and John's family.

. . .

The result was phenomenal! Once again, the family, friends, body of Christ and the community arose to the occasion and began leaving comments, encouraging the family and showing their level of faith and love.

A counter and a map were added to the blog site that tracked the number of visitors to the site and from what part of the world the messages came. At the beginning it was mostly Texas, but very quickly we saw that it was spreading throughout the United States. It did not take long before the map was being marked with visitors from other countries! Some folks just happened to "stumble" onto the blog while searching for other things on the Internet and became faithful prayer warriors. Some were doctors and nurses from McAllen that were with John during the first ten days and wanted to keep up with his progress. Over time, more than 110,000 hits were recorded on the blog site.

Prophetic words, visions and dreams started coming forth through the blog, and it was such a comfort to the family to know we were not walking through this alone. The only handbook or set of instructions we had to use was the Word of God. However, the Lord used the blog as an outreach, extending His arms around the world and loving everyone that came in contact with it. John Keller became a worldwide prayer vigil.

At the "Starting the Year Off Right Conference," earlier in January 2008, one of the words that came forth was about "gates." A statement was made that the gate you walk through may not be the gate you *want* to walk through. Again, Psalm 118 came up:

I shall not die, but live, And declare the works of the Lord. The Lord has chastened me severely, but He has not given me over to death. Open to me the gates of righteousness; I will go through them, And I will praise the Lord. This is the gate of the Lord, through which the righteous shall enter. I will praise You, For You have answered me, and have become my salvation.

Psalm 118:17-21 NKJV

We certainly did not want or ever expect to have to walk through the gate that was presented to us by John's accident. Regardless, we set our faces like flint and went through the gate, knowing we had God's promise that John would live and not die.

As we drove from the airport and through Houston, we passed MD Anderson Hospital, and Jan noticed a gate in the landscaping. She proclaimed, "Praise the Lord! Open to me the gates of Righteousness, I will go through them and I will Praise the Lord!" We arrived at The Methodist Hospital and quickly proceeded inside.

What a precious gift from God it was when we entered in the front doors of The Methodist Hospital! On the wall, behind the greeter's desk was a mural with a beautiful picture and the Scripture of Matthew 7:7 embedded in it. We knew we were in the right place and that God had brought us through the gate!

At the Neurosurgery ICU, we were greeted by a nurse who said, "We are glad you are here! We have been praying for you." They took us to John's bed, which was Bed 8! Praise God! The number "eight" in the Bible means *new beginnings*! John was immediately put on an arctic blanket to keep his body temperature low until his brain could regulate it to a normal level.

Through all of this, we had been hearing a message in the Spirit saying, "God is making a way of escape; the walls of your Jericho will come down." We just knew we had to start walking it out in God's time. You never know how much warfare you have to go through, but it is critical to keep seeking and knocking until you get the answer. When answers began to come, God opened a door, and we walked through it…all the way to Houston.

• • •

KEYS TO WALKING OUT A MIRACLE:

1. Walk carefully and come into proper alignment when your place of authority is changing.
2. Don't gripe or complain or focus on the "what if's," just keep praying and moving forward.
3. Seek opportunities to help others when you are in the midst of your own crisis.
4. Ask the Lord to reveal areas that you need to know about *before* they become a problem and then pray strategically.
5. Set your face like a flint and walk through whatever gate is set before you, knowing that God's promises never change.

Miracle Testimony

Heather McGuire Carr

There are times in life when you are exactly where God wants you to be even when the situation may seem terribly wrong. But the person God created you to be is so magnificently perfect for the hardship, all you can do is be a humble and willing servant. That is how I felt in this time with John. I have known John all my life. He is six months older than me, and our parents have always been best friends. Needless to say, when John was in his accident, it was as if it was my brother who was hurting. Our family knew where we were supposed to be: praying and helping in any way possible at the McAllen Medical Center.

My experience of John's accident varies a bit from others in that I am a registered nurse. In most cases, I am able to separate myself emotionally to do the nursing tasks needed. I was unable to do that in this situation. I was required to use all of the gifts God had given me to help, and because of this, I was rocked to the core. After not actively working as a nurse for several years, I felt rusty as I was thrown into this tragic and awesome calling. Each person affected by John's accident was called into a new place that was more than we had ever before experienced. If I have learned anything, it is that God does not need me to accomplish His purpose, but He wants me to be a part of His plan.

I was humbled. God wanted to use me: a family friend and an R.N. who had been placed in a neurology internship at M. D. Anderson Hospital, which at the time was not of interest to me. God gave me something I thought I did not want, and it ended up being the very experience that ten years later would help my family's dearest friends walk through the most difficult time of their lives. Only God knew that the knowledge and the people I had come in contact with along the way would help facilitate a miracle of godly proportions.

In the physical world, John would have been considered a lost cause, but the doctors had not met our God, the One who heals and was ready to show Himself in a mighty way. I love being a nurse because I get to watch the Hand of God. Healthcare providers are limited in what we can do, but I watch as God covers the gap between what mortal men can do and what He does.

"All is well" was our constant theme. That little phrase was everything to us in those early days. God had given that Word and He was confirming it every-where we looked. All was well because God was in control of the matter. I pray all of you who read this book will get a sense of not only God's magnificence, but the spiritual battle that was being fought for John's life. It was personal and it was spiritual. John's life will never be the same. Mine will not be either. God has called John, me and you to a purpose ordained by Him, set in motion by events we cannot control, affected by experiences we go through that are completed in His perfect timing. You may be experiencing a difficult time in your life right now, but "Be confident of this, that He who began a good work in you will carry it on to completion until the day of Christ Jesus." Phil. 1:6

Chapter 8

All Things Are Possible With God

April Keller

Arriving in Houston and walking into the Neurosurgery ICU at The Methodist Hospital, it was a crazy, scary and yet reassuring sight altogether to see John hooked up to every machine possible with three or more doctors or nurses watching over him. It was a very different scenario than where we had been in McAllen. We began with all the medical questioning and history about John, but I felt like we were in good hands. The doctor, to whom John's care was transferred, could tell we were tired and worn out. He assured us John was stable and encouraged us to go get some rest. So, we settled into a nearby hotel, got a late night dinner and tried to rest for an early start the next day.

After starting Wednesday, February 27th off with a quick breakfast and arriving in time for visiting hours, honestly I can't remember what happened that day. I just knew John was in better hands, and God was doing the rest. The team of doctors had worked through the night gathering information on John, and he was still sedated while they managed his pain. They installed a new pressure-reading device and a ventricular drain on his head. We were reminded again that John had now slipped into a real coma rather than a medically-induced coma. All we knew was that we had to keep pushing him forward and watch out for him as best we could.

Jennifer, John's sister, called Jan and shared a vision she had of John in his bed at The Methodist Hospital. In the vision, she could see that if he raised his head, he could see down the hall where the doors were open to him and behind them another set of doors that led to the outside. She, also, said she saw an elevator on the left. Jan was drawing out the diagram as Jennifer was telling her about it. Her vision was exactly how the hallway was laid out without Jennifer being there or having ever seen it. Once again, God was confirming that He knew just exactly what was going on, and He was in control. It was hard to wait, but we knew John's healing would fall into place in God's perfect timing.

We were able to spend some time with John as the visiting hours here were open most of the day. A volunteer greeted us in the waiting room, and Jan asked her why she volunteered here at the hospital. She responded, "About this time last year, I was right where you are today. My 23-year-old son had a tumor and had to have three surgeries. Today he is back at work in his office at the City of Houston and praising the Lord for his healing."

Jan said to her, "God's perfect timing makes all things beautiful. For such a time as this, God is right here with us and is providing exactly what we need. We are listening to the Lord and thanking Him for His ever present help in time of trouble."

• • •

Blog February 29, 2008 (Leap Year):

This is the day that the Lord has made. We will rejoice and be glad in it! John is responding to voices and touch but is still sedated and sleeping. They are going to perform two necessary procedures today, which are standard, but we still need to pray that they work together for John's good. We are still receiving confirmation from the words you all are sending and hearing from the Lord that John is going to rise up, wake up, and spring forth, and those are the words we are standing on. Thank you, JESUS!

• • •

By the first week in March, John was still sedated, but resting and healing. There were medical issues that needed prayer, such as swelling on the brain and fighting infection in John's body, but we knew John was getting the best care possible. The pressure on his brain had gone down and his vitals were looking great. The doctors had cut his ventilator back, and he was breathing 95% on his own.

We all wanted to believe that John could wake up at any time once the medication was stopped, but we had no idea how long this entire process was going to take. It was hard having my kids split between home and Houston, my husband in a coma, and not knowing what my future held. I sang to him and talked to him every day and told him what the boys were doing. I never once considered the possibility of John not coming back to us. We just kept pushing him forward and watching out for him.

I inquired about everything from the medication being given to John, to the tubes he was hooked up to, to what every monitor meant. I felt like I had to know what was going on at all times, because after all, this was John's life they were dealing with.

After reading the EEG (electroencephalogram), the doctor at The Methodist Hospital met with Jan, James, my mom and me. He said he was sorry to inform us that they could not give us much hope for John because of his severe traumatic brain injury. He went on to say that if John ever woke up or got out of bed, he would be in a wheelchair the rest of his life. The severity of the situation set in as we were told that, at best, John might be able to hold a regular, minimum-wage paying job but for sure not be able to resume his previous work as CEO of the family business. We thanked the doctor for taking John as his patient and told him that we would just have to rely on the Lord for His healing touch, and we would wait and see what the Lord has planned! The doctor agreed that God could do it.

When I heard this report, I was crushed. All John longed to do was work, and if he couldn't do what he was doing before, he would not be happy. This was so hard to take, and I had to put my faith in God in front of this doctor's words. From this point on, I decided that I had to forget what the doctors said as far as a diagnosis was concerned and just lean on God's promise. I walked out on one doctor telling us some of the same disturbing news.

The doctors told us this was going to be a long road, but the family knew that with God all things are possible! Plans were made immediately to begin physical therapy on John's upper body and to start taking him off his sedation. As the days passed, relationships began to form with John's nurses and even one special internist. He told me he prayed for John every day and wanted him to return to his boys. He was a sweet man that really pulled for us and watched over John carefully.

The rest of the week went pretty much the same. John was resting and healing. People were leaving comments from all over the United States on the blog that were full of prayers and praise! John had been off sedation, and everyone was waiting in anticipation of John waking up.

By our second week in ICU, Caden and my parents had come to stay with us. They watched Caden at the apartment while Jan, Dalton and I went to the hospital. Thankfully, God gave me a sweet, easy going baby that nursed well, slept at the hospital and smiled at everyone. Dalton brought much joy to me and to many others that were going through difficult times. Oddly enough, as time passed, Dalton reached all his baby milestones, like smiling, rolling over, sitting up, and he was ahead of his older brother at this age. It's funny, we always say God only gives you what you can handle, so he gave me an easy going, happy baby…but I think I would have preferred a cranky baby to a husband in a coma! But God didn't ask me, he just chose for me!

While John was in ICU, a trach was inserted because they didn't want the breathing tube down his throat to damage his vocal cords. These procedures were so foreign to me, but we knew God was in control and always prayed that He would guide the doctors' decisions and every move they made. God was faithful to do what we asked.

• • •

Blog March 3, 2008:

Psalm 91: (1) He who dwells in the shelter of the Most High will rest in the shadow of the Almighty. (2) I will say of the LORD, "He is my refuge and my fortress, my God, in whom I trust." Well, the Lord just keeps showing us His awesome power. Unknowingly to us, until we arrived this morning, they took John off of his sedation medication. They are playing praise and worship music to help stimulate him. We are praying that John will rise up and awaken. His CT scan came back positive, and he is still breathing above the respirator.

• • •

KEYS TO WALKING OUT A MIRACLE:

1. Be willing to wait for God's perfect time.
2. Put your faith in God in front of bad reports or impossible circumstances and just lean on God's promise.

Miracle Testimony

Keith Meschi

J ohn Keller's circumstances have deeply impacted my faith in Jesus Christ. John is living proof that God is still working miracles in people's lives. God has shown me through John's circumstances that if we believe God is good and just, He will show us these characteristics. The power of prayer was evident in John's miraculous healing. He is a miracle, and I am so grateful to God for giving John a second chance to let his light shine thru the power of his testimony. His testimony will further God's Kingdom and that is a beautiful thing. I hope this book reaches and touches the hearts of a multitude of people.

As vice-president of Wencar, Inc. and a vendor for the Keller family business, John and I have worked side-by-side for a number of years. I admire John for his integrity and humor, but most of all I am honored to call him my friend.

During a time of praise and worship at The Methodist Hospital in Houston on March 6, 2008, this song was birthed in my spirit for John:

Tell Us Your Story

WAKE UP JK AND TELL US THE STORY.

CAN YOU SIT UP AND BRAG ABOUT GOD'S GLORY?

TELL US JOHN, WHAT YOU'VE BEEN DREAMIN ABOUT!

LET ME GUESS, HMMM…WORKING OUT?

(Chorus)

TELL US YOUR STORY, ABOUT THE POWER OF GOD'S GLORY

DRIVEN BY HIS SPIRIT, HE'S THE ONE WHO GIVES IT.

TELL THE WORLD HOW YOUR LIFE WAS SPARED,

BY THE GREAT REDEEMER, DON'T BE SCARED.

JUST LIKE GOD CREATED MAN TO WALK,

GET UP TODAY AND START TO TALK.

WE WANT TO HEAR YOUR STORY ABOUT LIFE AND DEATH,

WE WANT TO HEAR HOW GOD SAVED YOUR LIFE,

AND SPARED YOUR BREATH.

TO REMAIN ON THIS GLOBE AND TELL US THE TRUTH

ABOUT JESUS AND WHAT HE DID IN YOU!

(Repeat Chorus)

GET UP TODAY AND OPEN THOSE EYES

OPEN THOSE EYES AND SEE THE SUNRISE.

TELL US YOUR STORY, THE POWER OF YOUR SPIRIT

DRIVEN BY THE ONE, JESUS CHRIST WHO GIVES IT.

TELL THE WORLD HOW YOU HIT THE CONCRETE
HOW GOD APPEARED TO YOU WHILE YOU WERE LYING IN
THE STREET
WE WANT TO KNOW, DO ANGELS HAVE WINGS?
ARE THEY DRESSED IN WHITE? CAN THEY REALLY SING?

(Repeat Chorus)

WE KNOW THE SPIRIT IS IN YOU TODAY,
SO GET UP DADDY AND LET'S GO PLAY.
GET UP JK AND STAND GREAT AND TALL,
STAND AND SPEAK OF ALL THE MIRACLES YOU JUST SAW.

YOUR LIFE WAS GIVEN TO BE A GREAT FATHER,
THE TRUTHS YOU KNOW;
WITH THE WORLD VIEWS DON'T BOTHER.
PRAISE GOD, PRAISE JESUS, PRAISE THE HEAVENLY ONE,
FOR THE GREAT WORK IN YOU THAT HE HAS JUST DONE.

(Repeat Chorus)

COME ON JOHN TELL US YOUR STORY!

Chapter 9

Standing Strong

James Keller

On Sunday, March 9, 2008, there was excitement and enthusiasm in the air. God was about to do something because His presence was so heavy in John's room. John had a special visitor, one of the high school coaches from the Rio Grande Valley. When I asked John to blink his eyes — he had not opened his eyes since the accident — miraculously, although he didn't open his eyes, he fluttered his eyelids and squinted/blinked! Then we asked him to do it five times, and we counted them off as he did it. This was a big step forward because he did it on command and not just spontaneously.

For the rest of the late morning and afternoon, John took deep breaths and stretched his shoulders and arms. He was definitely showing signs of working hard to wake up. We knew John had to take baby steps each day all in God's perfect timing.

The next week began with a day full of x-rays and scans. John was doing well to respond to commands and encouragement to blink and breathe above his ventilator, but he had also developed pneumonia. The doctor was treating it aggressively but the antibiotics weren't working. He said a new round of stronger Penicillin™ antibiotics should do the trick. As a child, John had an allergic reaction to Penicillin™ so we had to believe in faith that John would not have a reaction to these stronger antibiotics, and he didn't.

The doctors decided to take John back into surgery and put in a shunt to drain off the excess CSF (cerebrospinal fluid) his body was producing. The neurosurgeon said this might put John a week behind in starting rehab, but he felt it would be better to take care of it now.

By 5:30 pm, John was out of surgery and all appeared to be well. Everyone believed this would help him move to the next level of recovery and healing. One of John's doctors told us when he entered John's room that morning, he called out John's name, and John jumped - like someone does when he is startled! Thank you Jesus! The doctors really liked the progress they were seeing.

For the first three months, Jan and April never went home. While John was in ICU, they were always there, and I came to Houston on the weekends. One weekend, John's sister, Jené and her husband, Jon, were following me back to the Valley. The Lord had been so awesome to speak to us in different ways through this journey with John. As we were headed south on the highway, I spotted a huge billboard across the expressway. It had a white background with black letters with only two words "STAND STRONG" posted on it. Then coming into town we saw another sign that read, "YOU ARE IN REALLY, REALLY GOOD HANDS." Thank God He can encourage us even on the expressway of life.

Walking through those difficult days after John's accident, I struggled at times. Jan kept saying, "Don't go by what you *see*; go by what you *know!*" When the accident first occurred, I couldn't go to the accident scene because I knew my faith would have been shattered by what I would have seen – the blood, the lines on the highway showing where the bike parts were scattered and where John landed. I couldn't have handled it.

John's grandfather went to the accident site the day after it occurred and found a shredded t-shirt in the brush with the word "Finisher" on it. It was thought to be the shirt John was wearing at the time of the accident and had been discarded when the emergency medical technicians cut it off John to start treating him. To this day, John does not remember ever owning that t-shirt, and April agrees that he did not have a shirt like that either.

His grandfather may have found someone else's shirt, but God used it so the family would know that John would be a finisher of his race, that John was still running his race, and that God has plans for him to be there to raise his two small sons into godly young men. It didn't matter if the shirt belonged to John or not. We needed a Word to hold onto that John would be a finisher. We claimed Hebrews 12:2: *"looking unto Jesus, the author and finisher of our faith, who for the joy that was set before Him endured the cross, despising the shame, and has sat down at the right hand of the throne of God."*

We had bracelets made for everyone to wear declaring, John Keller Is Healed In Jesus' Name, and with the Scripture, Hebrews 12:2 on it.

Jan has such an unwavering faith that at times I had to link onto her faith to pull me through the things I saw with my eyes. My faith is activated and confirmed by signs and wonders, such as the significance of numbers, signs on billboards, a shredded t-shirt, etc.

I wasn't there with John all the time in Houston as I had to be in McAllen during the week to oversee our family business operations, but people I came in contact with shared some faith-building insights with me from time to time. I met a man from the ambulance service in McAllen who told me that when the EMS team loaded John into the ambulance, they did not radio the emergency room to have blood on hand because they thought John would be DOA (dead on arrival). He, also, told me that John's body was so twisted from the impact of how he landed on the pavement after flying 150 feet in the air, that his legs were literally wrapped around his head. Can you even imagine a 6'5" man twisted like a pretzel? BUT GOD...preserved John's life. That was a faith-builder for me.

The calls, prayers, Scriptures, and comments coming from friends, family and even strangers on the blog and in other ways were strengthening and helped propel us through each day.

> *But we continue to preach because we have the same kind of faith the psalmist had when he said, "I believed in God, so I spoke. We know that God, who raised the Lord Jesus, will also raise us with Jesus and present us to himself together with you."*
>
> II Corinthians 4:13-14 NLT

The month of March was something like a rollercoaster ride with many ups and downs. John came off the respirator and sedation but then had to go back on for a while because of congestion in his lungs. Over time he was able to come off the sedation medication, and the doctors said his pupils were beginning to dilate, which was an indication he could wake up anytime. A feeding tube was inserted so he could begin to receive protein shakes without the uncomfortable tube in his mouth. At times, we would see that he was moving his head and feet and was squinting/blinking, even though his eyes were still closed.

By mid-month, therapy was progressing, and John was able to sit in a reclining bed/chair for increasing periods of time. Everyone agreed it was time to leap forward with the milestones John was being expected to accomplish, and the doctors felt that The Institute for Research and Rehabilitation (TIRR) in Houston would be the best place for him.

April had heard about TIRR from one of the caregivers at The Methodist Hospital. She took a tour just to check it out, but getting into TIRR was like a bad waiting game. They would come and evaluate John and then inform us later if he would be approved to go, and then that depended on if a bed was available. We were turned down once because John was still fighting brain fever, and we were told this could take months to get better as it was controlled by the part of the brain that was injured.

Many challenges had to be overcome to get John accepted at TIRR. April was instrumental in getting John weaned off the respirator and breathing room air on his own through his trach. She knew exactly what the machine would do for him and closely monitored how much of the breathing John was doing on his own. If there happened to be a new or different respiratory therapist on duty, she made sure the therapist knew what to do and not to give him full oxygen. She just knew he could do it and pushed the therapists so before John left ICU, he was breathing room air only. That was another of the stipulations for being accepted at TIRR.

Then I received an e-mail that simply said "NEXT STEP." We did not fully understand what it meant, but as we prayed, the Lord revealed that it was time for a new process to begin and time to get John to his next place. This was exactly what the staff at the hospital had been telling Jan earlier in the day. It was time to move John to rehab within the next few days. This was confirmation to my prayers because God was ready to do a new thing in John. God is so good! He was leading us step by step. I believe we had felt some of the fellowship of Christ's suffering, and now I prayed to see the power of his resurrection knowing the promise — God told me that He did not take Isaac and that He was not going to take John! Praise the Lord!

There were so many miracles in this process, and it was because of everyone's faithful prayers and crying out to heaven. There was a sound coming up from the earth into the heavens and our wonderful God and Savior, Jesus Christ, was hearing it. I thank God that this will continue to get louder and then transition into praise as we shout for joy for the healing in John's body to be brought to completion and he holds April and his boys again!

Then John began having what they call brain fevers and sweats. His doctors indicated that the fever was not a problem, and it would go away once the area of his brain that controls the body temperature has healed. John just needed more time to heal. It was decided to leave John at The Methodist Hospital for a few more days to allow his body to rest and heal, before making the move to TIRR. Everyone kept praying. By now people in other countries were starting to read the blog.

• • •

Blog March 20, 2009:

Just got word from Jan that John's fever is lower and he is not having any of the brain sweats. He was sitting up in a chair this morning for over three hours and totally relaxed, not tense. He is assimilating the protein now, and his skin color looks great! They have weaned him off the IV feeding of TPN, and he is accepting the nutrients from his feeding tube. The nutritionist came by and she wanted to make sure that we bring John back so she can rejoice in the miracle too. She said she was real encouraged to see how well John's skin was doing. So we shared with her how we are covering every single area of John's body in prayer and that we would be sure to add his skin to the list. What a blessed day from the LORD! Thank you Father! Just wanted to give the great news! Praise God! Keep on praying, heaven is hearing and God is healing!

• • •

On March 23rd, Resurrection Sunday, Jan and Jon Byron, John's brother-in-law, and I were in John's room around 2:00 pm. John seemed to be alert though his eyes were still closed. I asked him to squeeze my hand, and he did it three times. I can't tell you the joy we felt when he did it. It was such a blessing as we had asked God to give us a sign for good that the enemies of God would be ashamed. The Lord was showing us His great love for John and all of us through this walk of faith. We learned that He is in all the little things that go unnoticed, and in this part of our journey we began looking so much harder for the Lord and His direction.

On this Resurrection Sunday, we considered the resurrection of our precious Lord Jesus in that there was no one there to lay hands on Him, etc. What power our Lord has over death and hell. Because He rose, we have hope; our hope is in our Lord. We are looking for that blessed hope and lay hold of a better, lively hope in Him. We hope in His Word and thank Him for loving us so much that He would die for us. We truly serve an awesome God!

· · ·

KEYS TO WALKING OUT A MIRACLE:

1. Allow God to speak to you in different or unusual ways through your journey.
2. Watch for the unexpected and rejoice in all things.
3. Cover everything big and small in prayer.

Miracle Testimony

Stephanie Carroll

I t is understood that if you are working in health care, you should never expect the mundane and always be ready for a surprise. My surprise came when I met John Keller's family in the waiting room of the Neuro ICU. I didn't know then, but this patient was about to completely defeat the odds, and his family would change my view of faith in my heavenly Father as John healed.

I work at The Methodist Hospital as a Patient Advocate, and I was just doing every-day rounds to check on the families of the Neuro Intensive Care Unit when I met the Kellers and learned of our mutual belief in God and his power to heal. But I knew John's prognosis wasn't good, and I'd been with too many families with the same faith who had different fates. For months the NICU staff and I watched the Keller family live a different faith than I had ever seen. We never saw fear. We never saw doubt. We always saw hope. This family would not be moved, and they would tell anyone who would listen. What a ministry they made out of a devastating circumstance.

I visited John occasionally after he was transferred out of our hospital, and every time I saw immense improvements. I often left laughing and saying, "God, You're really going to do this!" But the Keller's knew that all along. I have never *witnessed the power of prayer like I did with the Keller family. They changed my hope in Jesus from ordinary to unwavering. I have many days when I ask God "Why?" I almost always hear Jan saying, "We have to see with our faith the end result." Just like they did and still do.*

Stephanie Carroll
Patient Liaison I
The Methodist Hospital
Houston, TX

Chapter 10

Next Step to a Miracle

April Keller

I felt like John needed to be at The Institute for Rehabilitation and Research (TIRR), and I know Jan and James did too. Finally, John's last days at The Methodist Hospital were coming to an end, and he was ready to move on to the next level. TIRR did not have a bed for John yet, but another rehab facility did and that was where we thought we were headed.

Jan went to the hospital early Monday morning the day after Easter, while I stayed at the apartment to spend some time with the boys. Then I received a call from the case worker at TIRR saying I needed to come sign some papers for John's transfer. This made our day! We were going to TIRR, one of the top rehab facilities in the nation! God was surely in control!

TIRR can trace its roots back to the early 1950s when polio was at the height of its epidemic in the United States. William A. Spencer, M.D., established one of the first polio treatment centers in the nation in Houston. With the discovery of the polio vaccine in the 1960s, the expertise developed by this nationally recognized respiratory center was applied to rehabilitating catastrophically injured patients. Much of what was learned in treating polio survivors would prove very valuable and applicable to other disabling injuries and illnesses.

On May 30, 1959, the Texas Institute for Rehabilitation and Research was formally dedicated and began accepting patients. In 1978, the hospital changed its name to The Institute for Rehabilitation and Research. Known today as TIRR Memorial Hermann, Dr. Spencer changed the way society and healthcare responded to disability and rehabilitation. Today, TIRR changes lives by improving outcomes, offering hope and maximizing independence for those impacted by disabling injury or illness.[1]

I rode with John in the ambulance on the short ride over to TIRR, which would be his home for the next few months. Once we arrived, we were taken to the sixth floor to wait and get registered. This was a scary transition because we were going from ICU meaning one nurse to one-to-two patients, to one nurse for five-to-seven patients. It meant having our own room with no curtain. Although John was stable, he still was asleep, just recently breathing on his own, and also immobile, so this was terrifying for me. Jan volunteered to stay the night with John to make sure he was taken care of so that I could go back to the apartment to be with our boys.

Our boys seemed to be handling everything pretty good considering they were used to being with me all the time and seeing their dad in the evenings. Now it was no more dad and only a little bit of me. I felt so bad for them and was so pulled between being with the kids and with John. Also, I didn't want them to get any bad vibes off of me because of the situation we were in. I know kids feed off their parent's emotions, and I wanted to make sure I didn't crumble in front of them, so I never did. I am normally a very even keel person, who doesn't have highs and lows, but these weren't normal circumstances. Somehow I managed to stay this way throughout this difficult journey I was on. I know it was from the many people praying for my strength, courage, and patience that I was able to get up every morning and smile and laugh with our boys, and then head to the hospital to be with John and try to awaken him.

TIRR brought many changes for us. John was going to be dressed every day in workout clothes - no more hospital gowns. He would be in a wheelchair every day, not a bed! All these steps were in the right direction, just different. The daily therapy sessions focused on one main goal: to help him wake up...WAKE UP JOHN!!

• • •

Blog March 24, 2008:

John is at TIRR in a room on the 6th floor. Jan says the floor has been newly remodeled, and it is such a nice place. They are very excited to have John and look forward to working with him. He will start with his therapy tomorrow.

Once John was getting situated at TIRR in his new room, his physical therapist and Jan were talking. Jan was sharing with her that we believe the Lord is going to work a big miracle in John's life and that he will be restored completely. Her response was, "Yes, you are right. We see miracles all the time around here. We'll be working with a patient who is asleep, and suddenly that patient wakes up and instantly starts reading my name tag."

Thank you for your prayers over John as he starts this new phase. They are going to start right away with physical and occupational therapy even though he is still asleep. We think this is to really stimulate him to wake up and open his eyes. Our prayers are that the Lord would cover John with peace, patience, and understanding that this is all for his good.

In all these things we are more than conquerors through him who loved us.

Romans 8:37 NKJV

• • •

KEYS TO WALKING OUT A MIRACLE:
1. Adjust to change, it's inevitable.
2. Share your testimony as it unfolds: It builds your faith and the faith of others.
3. Remember: God knows exactly where you are and He is right there with you.

Miracle Testimony

Pat Simpson

Never would I wish a trial like John's on anyone or their family, but as John's aunt, what a blessing it has been to see God do miracles each day. Through this time, I have seen it truly as a test for the entire family. We have all been through the test of the fire, but we have all grown as a result. Many families pray believing as ours did for miracles, but ultimately it is in God's hands who shall receive. The one thing I have learned from this experience is that if you are blessed enough to receive God's miracle, then it is your duty to share what God has done with others. "Declare the works of the Lord," Psalm 118:17. Our God is still a God of Miracles

Chapter 11

Pushing Forward

Jan Keller

The doctors and therapy team at TIRR immediately set specific goals for John and pushed forward, which is exactly what the family wanted! The speech therapist began working with John using a new device that worked with his trach so he would be able to talk with the trach still in place. All IV lines were removed, and his trach downsized because he was breathing so well on his own. A cast was created for John's left foot to make sure it stayed in the correct position. The cast was cut in half vertically and fastened with buckles, and it could be uncomfortable to wear. The rehab staff knew the patients tolerated the casts better at night when they were resting. Through all of this, John was still in a coma.

During all John's therapy sessions, they exercised his arms and legs to try and keep the muscles from fading away. The therapist at TIRR tried anything and everything from putting ice on his face, under his armpits or even down his pants to try and get a reaction from John. It was definitely challenging because progress for John was not always apparent, and we were seeing signs of muscle atrophy and spasticity.

As each day passed, the Lord continued to strengthen and heal John with more miracles being confirmed. During John's speech therapy session, the therapist opened John's eyes and then clapped loudly in front of his face. John flinched confirming what they were thinking: John can see! So from that point on, they began taping John's eyes open during therapy so that he was being stimulated through his sense of sight. Another good sign was that John began trying to lift his head, as if to try to sit up. This is something that is not usually seen until after months of rehabilitation!

Word came that John was being moved into a new room – Room 310. The nurse told me that we were moving into the "Miracle Room."

I replied, "That is great! We are all about miracles, but why do you call this the miracle room?"

The nurse explained that the young man in this room left here after four months of rehabilitation to go to an independent living home. He was doing very well walking and talking. He, also, had a ten-month-old son and wife that had been with him all the time.

I said, "How great is that! God is moving and directing our every move. He is divinely appointing our steps."

The family of the previous patient in that room wanted to be sure we knew about this being the "Miracle Room." I told the nurse to be sure to convey to the family that we believe in miracles, too.

John looks great! April was doing therapy on his left arm and hand, and he squeezed James' hand and then squeezed it again really hard. Praise the Lord! He was sitting up in his wheelchair and looking really comfortable. When April opened his left eye, he followed me as I moved my head left to right. Oh, what a gracious God we have! The most astonishing thing about miracles is that they happen! We continued to cry out to the Lord, intercede and move forward. We have a great God and nothing is too difficult for Him! We want to see God's Kingdom come to earth as it is in heaven.

I also tell you this - if two or more of you agree down here on earth concerning anything you ask for, my Father in heaven will do it for you.

Matthew 18:19 NKJV

The month of April brought a lot of activity for John. The techs helped John every morning to get up, get dressed and be up out of bed, either in a chair or a wheelchair. His schedule allowed him to get out of his chair for a one-hour rest break mid day.

We moved into an apartment just minutes away from TIRR. April's dad and step-mom stayed with us to help keep the boys in a home-away-from-home atmosphere. I loved going early in the morning to help with John's routine because that was so John – he just loved routine! So, we thought, how much better to start that all over just the way he was before the accident! By eight o'clock in the morning, he was up in a wheelchair, ready to go for the day.

April's dad asked me why I wanted to go so early in the morning since John wasn't even awake yet. I said, "Because John is so much more alert and rested in the morning, and I love preparing him physically and spiritually for his day."

All of the therapists kept working toward the goal to try to get John to wake up. They even taped John's eyes open to see if that helped. April worked right along with the therapists day after day. Even after therapy sessions ended, she continued doing range of motion with John, the more the better, she figured it couldn't hurt! For a long time we didn't see any progress, but we never gave up and neither did they. That was the amazing part, they encouraged us without fail, and we knew John just wasn't healed enough yet to wake up.

Then, little by little, things started to happen. John did two bicep curls on his own. He pushed away the therapist when she pulled his arm hair. He was holding his head up by himself. He started making noises, and even turned his head toward the TV when a basketball game was on. Then while I was brushing his teeth, he lifted his left arm to try to get me to stop messing with his mouth. This was so awesome because he used his left arm! Up to now, it had always been his right arm that he preferred to use.

Meanwhile, at home, James was driving by the Baptist Church that is close to our home, and he noticed the words on their outdoor sign, "Sometimes we see better with our eyes closed." James immediately started praising God saying "Thank you, Father, for your confirmation that there is perfect timing to everything you are doing in John's body to bring about his complete healing and total restoration."

• • •

Blog April 10, 2008:

During the night the Lord woke us up and gave us specific instructions concerning how we needed to pray through for John.

When Jan got to John's room, the sweet Christian girl that worked in Radiology came by to pray for John. It was an awesome prayer that included everything we believed the Lord for John's healing. In physical therapy, the student intern shared how she had heard a testimony of a preacher that had been in a coma for three months and could remember so much of what was said around him during his sleep and the warfare he was going through during his coma until he awoke.

Jan began to read out of John's personal Promise Bible that he would walk in newness of life. During that reading, there was a knock on the door. It was his physical therapist telling us that the doctor had given clearance for John to begin weight bearing exercises. So, today during PT time, they placed John on an incline table and started at a 10 degree incline. Then they increased the incline every few minutes; all the time checking his blood pressure and respirations to verify that he was tolerating the exercise well. After 30 minutes, they had gotten John to a 60 degree incline! Jan could tell by the expression on the therapists' faces that they were taken back and really couldn't believe what they were seeing. So she asked them, "This is good, right?" And they replied, "Yes, really, really good. Usually patients can only endure about 10 minutes their first day and definitely don't make it to 60 degrees." WOW! HOW GREAT IS OUR GOD!

John is now completely off the insulin (which they have had him on since he was in ICU because of all the IVs with glucose) and his blood work numbers have been great.

They gave us homework for John. We are to splash him with water and see what reaction we get from him. It came back to us; that is exactly how we used to wake John up during high school. We got a laugh out of that; and we turned it into a time of anointing John with God's grace, splashing him 5 (God's number for grace) times. We received a good report from the doctors, and they are very pleased with his progress!

John just completed his morning therapy session. The therapist liked the range of motion in his arms. John squeezed the therapist's hand with his right hand! Praise the Lord! One of John's nurses said she was so excited to get the new patient because she had already been praying for John (before she even met him). She is a believer and is eager to see the Lord work a miracle in John's life. It is such a blessing to be surrounded by people who hook up with our faith and just make it stronger! We are believing GOD!

• • •

John had a special visit from his orthopedic surgeon in the Valley. When Dr. Fulp walked into the room, he went right to John and introduced himself. He asked John to blink and John did it. John's eyes were still closed at this time, but he definitely fluttered his eyelids in a blinking motion. So Dr. Fulp said, "Okay, John that was good, but I want you to blink twice this time." John did it! Dr. Fulp said, "John, now move your mouth." John did it! Dr. Fulp exclaimed, "John is a miracle! I cannot believe what I've just seen, and the responses we got from John!"

Although we were never able to pinpoint a specific day when it happened, as we began to see his eyes open even a little bit, was when the therapy staff considered John had come out of the coma. We learned that his blank stare did not mean he wasn't awake. It was very hard to watch, but we knew we were speaking to his spirit and believed he was in there trying to respond.

One day April and I held John's eyes open and showed him a video of Caden. He really focused on it, so we showed it to him four times. We prayed over him this afternoon, speaking to his spirit man and commanding it to come to a new level of awareness, because God is giving him new orders - WAKE UP! He needs to hear those commands and follow them. We are continuing to pray against complications, seizures, his medicines to work for his good, and that the doctors, nurses, and therapists be directed by the Lord in caring for and treating John.

In the middle of April, John started vocalizing and making sounds. He had begun holding his head up for quite a while as well. The most exciting thing to see was that John was beginning to hold his eyes open! At first, he held his eyes half–way open for about 30 seconds. This was after his therapist had opened his eyes to say "Hi" to him. Over the course of weeks, John went from having his eyes about one-quarter of the way open without any help, to the mid-line, and then we could see the iris of his eyes!

A goal was set by John's occupational therapist who wanted John to be able to hold a wash cloth in his hand and move it up to his face as if he was wiping off his face. This was an important progress identifier to continue therapy at TIRR.

On one particular morning during this time span, I walked out to catch the bus to TIRR. It was a beautiful morning and in my spirit was a great sense of expectancy. I started praying for John immediately and thanking the Lord for all the things He was going to do in John today. When I got to his room, occupational therapy was already there working with John, and I pointed out how alert and responsive he was. His nurse said he was even more alert and his eyes were one-half of the way open earlier that morning. So during therapy with his eyes taped open, they noticed he was tracking very well and more than usual.

From there, John went to physical therapy and was placed on the incline board at 60 degrees. The therapists started talking among themselves and kind of laughing. I asked what was going on, and they told me in their morning meeting they had set a goal for John today. While on the incline board, they wanted him to hold his head up by himself for 30 seconds.

Well, he blew that goal out of the water because he was already at seven minutes and still going strong. Hallelujah!

John was showing improvement each and every day and working so hard to get his eyes open. He opened both eyes enough to be able to see both pupils (2/3 open) in sensory integration therapy. It was the most anyone had seen at that point. Both of his legs were in casts now to help keep full range of motion with his ankles. It was so wonderful that they were doing all this anticipatory medicine ahead of any of these issues even being a problem.

> *God is not a man, that he should lie, nor a son of man, that he should change his mind. Does he speak and then not act? Does he promise and not fulfill?*
>
> Numbers 23:19 NKJV

By the end of April, the therapists in physical therapy assisted John in standing up. They didn't use the incline board or any other apparatus; they just helped him stand up. He couldn't pull himself up, but he held himself up with their help - to balance him. They were very impressed because he knew how to lock his knees and hold his head up. He tracked April with his eyes as she walked around. It is exciting to see John working so hard and making steady progress.

• • •

Blog April 30, 2008:

We have an answer to prayer to share with you. We have been praying in agreement with you for the Lord to grant grace and favor concerning the discharge date for John. We have asked the Lord to let John stay at TIRR. Well, yesterday, the doctor said she had approved all therapy for John to be stepped up. She felt John would do fine, and with all the positive responsiveness she had been seeing, it would only help him move forward. So, today the doctor came back and said she just wanted to let us know **our discharge date has been moved to June 21st**. This is wonderful news. The Lord is faithful and just. Thank you for answering our prayers. What a great God we serve! Thank you all for joining with us and continuing to lift John up in prayer.

• • •

KEYS TO WALKING OUT A MIRACLE:

1. Remember: The most astonishing thing about miracles is that they happen!
2. Prepare both physically and spiritually for each day.
3. Watch the little things add up to big miracles.

Miracle Testimony

Sharee Britt

John Keller and his family truly define the word inspirational. He is a walking miracle and a testament that nothing is impossible for those who believe. John's recovery, after his accident seemed impossible in the natural...But God! The Keller family had fervent faith, and when faced with a battle that many would not have had the strength to fight, they fought on John's behalf and won.

When I first met John at TIRR in Houston, he was unable to do anything on his own. He didn't have the strength to sit up, stand, talk or even eat. From a therapist's point of view, John was totally dependent on others to perform the simplest task that many of us take for granted. But his family was always there going the extra mile for him. They went above and beyond doing what needed to be done to help John get a second chance at life.

At TIRR, we often suggest that the families of dependent patients bring them to a daily exercise class that allows them to use equipment that assists them with standing or that moves their arms or legs for them until they gain the strength to do it own their own. There are very few families that actually take the suggestion to heart, and then there are the Keller's. John's mother, Jan, would bring him into the exercise class every day and smile until she could find someone to help her get John set up on the equipment that his therapist's thought would help him get better. It was no easy task getting John's six-foot-plus body into the standing frame, but every day around 2 o'clock you could find Jan and John in the gym using the standing frame or the MotoMed to get his legs stronger. If it wasn't Jan, it was April. They took turns traveling to Houston to care for John and to make sure he was doing everything possible to get better.

I will never forget my first encounter with Jan. I was running the 2 o'clock exercise class, and she asked for my help to get John standing up in the frame. Once John was up and on his feet, Jan and I started talking. She commented on a bracelet I was wearing that says, "And Lo, I am with you always." Our conversation turned into a touching discussion of her faith in God and how she trusted in Him to heal John. She told me that the initials of all the members of her immediate family were JCK, which stood for Jesus Christ is King. It was that faith and the prayers of those who were constantly lifting John up in prayer that made his recovery and his awesome story possible.

I recall working with John on several occasions in therapy. It never ceases to amaze me that my first encounter with John involved me helping him into a frame that totally assisted him with standing when he was unable to stand on his own two feet. Our last session ended with him walking down the halls of the hospital so fast that April and I could barely keep up with him. He is truly a walking miracle, and it is stories like John's that make my job so gratifying.

Since his full recovery, John often visits the hospital, and it is so wonderful to see the staff crowding around him to marvel at his amazing progress. On one such visit, John shared with me his desire to write this book. I told him what a *great idea I thought it was and that it was sure to be a best seller. I, also, said he should get ready, because it would definitely be made into a movie as well. We laughed, and at that moment, I knew John Keller was back. I didn't know him before the accident, but I can tell he had a great personality. It has returned, along with his strength to walk, talk and even run. I am honored to know him and his family now, and I thank them for allowing me to see what a real family and faith are all about. They are truly an inspiration!*

Sharee Britt, Occupational Therapist
TIRR/Memorial Hermann

Chapter 12

Grace Abounds

James Keller

We are so thankful! Thankful to have a loving God! A God big enough to carry our burdens, hurts, and worries! A God big enough to answer our every prayer! A God big enough to heal us! A God big enough to restore us! A God big enough to heal John! A God big enough to restore John! Thank you, Lord; even though we may not understand all the intricate details of how Your plan fits together, You are still on the throne! You are still the Mighty One! You are the Everlasting Father, Prince of Peace, Lion of Judah! And we can rest in You knowing that You are God alone! We love you, Lord! We wholeheartedly love you.

As May 2008 began, we were reminded that May is the fifth month of the year and the number "five" in the Bible means *grace*. Grace, sometimes referred to as "God's unmerited favor," is one of, if not, *the* enduring theme of the Bible.

In Genesis, Chapter 17, God sealed his unconditional promises to Abram by the covenant of circumcision and by changing his name to Abraham. In the Hebrew this involved adding one letter to Abram's name - the fifth letter of the Hebrew alphabet. Sarai, Abram's wife, also had her name changed to Sarah by the addition of the fifth letter of the Hebrew alphabet."[1]

In Exodus, Chapter 30, we see that the recipe for the holy anointing oil consisted of five fine spices:

> *God spoke to Moses: Take the best spices: twelve and a half pounds of liquid myrrh; half that much, six and a quarter pounds, of fragrant cinnamon; six and a quarter pounds of fragrant cane; twelve and a half pounds of cassia—using the standard Sanctuary weight for all of them—and a gallon of olive oil. Make these into holy anointing oil, a perfumer's skillful blend.*
>
> Exodus 30: 22-45 THE MESSAGE

In I Samuel 17:40, we see that David picked up five smooth stones before he went out to slay the Philistines, one for Goliath and one for each of Goliath's four brothers.

> *Then he took his staff in his hand; and he chose for himself five smooth stones from the brook, and put them in a shepherd's bag, in a pouch which he had, and his sling was in his hand. And he drew near to the Philistine.*
>
> 1 Samuel 17:40 NKJV

And let us not forget, the five wounds of Christ that were the five piercing wounds inflicted upon Jesus during His crucifixion:

- Two of the wounds were through either His hands or His wrists, where nails were inserted to affix Jesus to the cross-beam of the cross on which He was crucified.
- Two were through Jesus' feet where the nails passed through both to the vertical beam.
- The final wound was in the side of Jesus' chest, where, according to the New Testament, His body was pierced by a lance in order to be sure that He was dead.

So, as the month of May unfolded, we began to see grace all around us: grace in the eyes of the hospital staff, the insurance company, all of the therapists, the nurses and the people praying at home and around the world for us.

> *No wonder we are happy in the Lord! For we are trusting the Lord, let your constant love surround us (John), for our hopes are in you alone."*
>
> Psalms 33:21-22 NKJV

• • •

Blog May 5, 2008:

Our prayers are availing much! Today, John spent more time with his mouth closed than ever before. This is such an answer to prayer! Thank you for praying in agreement with us. In fact, he actually had his lips puckered up around a straw today in sensory therapy. This weekend April put Dalton on John's lap and during the entire time Dalton was sitting there, John never tensed or toned his muscles. He was relaxed with his muscles at rest the entire time. What a blessing to see he is so sensitive to his son and the loving touch he has for Dalton. In physical therapy they stood John up again today. He did exactly what they were looking for, locked his knees and held his head up

• • •

John was given a swallowing test, and he passed it with flying colors. They gave him room temperature barium as this is more challenging to swallow than when used already cold or warmed up. When it was going down his throat, it started to go down the wrong tube. But John cleared his throat and the barium moved and started going down the right tube. They said he did very well, and they were impressed to see he made a conscious decision to clear his throat. As a reward, his speech therapist gave him ice cream – and a lot of it! John did very well with it and loved it! Next, they began moving on to pureed meals through the pegtube. How exciting it is to be telling of the miracles that the Lord is working in John's body! John is springing forth, leaping forward, and receiving his healing!

Then something exciting happened! John's eyes were almost all the way open! This was the first time we had seen that! It was so encouraging. John was moving forward in his healing!

May 11 was Mother's Day, and Jan said, "This was the best day ever because I had the greatest gift! John was here with us and every day is getting better and better."

John went on his first outing to tour the Reliant Stadium grounds with the TIRR therapists and April. They visited the suites and the weight room, and he had his eyes open for much of the tour.

As Jan and April came into John's room one morning, they could tell John was experiencing some pain. A look came over his face, and they said to him, "We know you are hurting, and we are trying to figure it out. We are fighting for you, and we know you are trying to tell us how to help you."

At first it was thought that John was experiencing "brain fevers" or "brainstorming" once again. His blood pressure was elevated, and he was sweating and had the shakes so bad it was decided to cut the cast off his leg in case it was causing the pain. With pain medication, he started to relax and his blood pressure came down. The family dug into the Scriptures:

> *He who dwells in the secret place of the Most High shall abide*
> *under the shadow of the Almighty.*
>
> Psalm 91:1 NKJV

Jan prayed, "Lord, allow John to abide under your shadow, protected, covered, and safe from all pain, harm, and fear. Direct the doctors and nurses as they treat and administer medicine to John. We agree that all meds would work for John's good. We love you, Lord, and thank you for the healing and restoration you are working in every area of John's body. Amen."

John endured fighting high blood pressure, sweating, high pulse and pain for several days. April and Jan kept asking for more urinalysis testing because they were seeing sediment in the catheter bag, but the test kept coming back negative for any urinary tract infection, which is a common event in bedridden patients. The doctor ordered John to complete bed rest because of the stress on his body. No one could figure out what was causing the pain that John was experiencing.

Jan and April were giving him lots of water because of the blood work results. They knew that an elevation of the Creatinine BUN numbers indicates that the patient could be dehydrated, and they had seen that in John, over and over again.

A new CT scan of his head and abdominal areas did not reveal anything, and, in fact, this was a good report in its own merit. However, it did not explain why his blood pressure was high, as well as his pulse, and that he was running a low fever and sweating.

April went to visit him during the late afternoon. John was awake, eyes wide open, and very alert and aware. She was talking with him and saw him shed a tear.

Within a day or two, they tried to return John to his scheduled therapy because he seemed to be doing better. His legs were recast in physical therapy, but his pulse spiked up, and he began sweating profusely this time. The techs were giving John showers two-to-three times, day and night for the muscle toning to try to get him to relax. Each time, they had to change the sheets from all of John's sweating. It was decided to put him back in bed and wait for the doctor to resolve this. The doctor finally identified the problem. An abdominal scan showed bladder stones.

. . .

Jennifer, John's sister, had come to visit for the weekend, but it was difficult for her to watch John who was obviously in so much pain.

Jennifer said, "I just kept strong in the Lord, praying and believing for him. Now that the problem was identified, they could address it. John was feeling much better in a very short period of time. His blood pressure was lower, but his pulse was still elevated a little. We got him up in the chair, gave him a shave and did some morning stretches. He definitely felt better because he was really vocalizing, but the sounds he was making were not groans and hurting sounds, so this was great! He was moving his left hand quite a bit. I did a lot of close eye-to-eye contact, holding his hand and speaking to him and his spirit. I told him how much he is loved, that everything was OK and everyone was taken care of, especially April, Caden, and Dalton. I assured him that Jesus was healing him - every single inch of his body was being restored, reconnected, reborn, and replaced."

"I began to get teary eyed, and then John shed another tear. So I just reassured him that he was in the Lord's hands and everything was OK. Jesus is healing John and we are seeing the evidence of it more each day. Thank you Lord!"

> *I tell you the truth, if you had faith even as small as a mustard*
> *seed, you could say to this mountain, "Move from here to there,"*
> *and it would move. Nothing would be impossible.*
>
> Matthew 17:20 NKJV

• • •

Jan Keller

It was determined that surgery was necessary to go in and capture the bladder stones that were causing John so much pain. The day started off early for John. He had to be at the outpatient surgery center for the procedure by 8:00 am. Because of the anesthesia, we were not allowed to feed him anything that morning. He did wonderful and was wide awake during the ambulance ride.

April called and talked to John over the phone. During their conversation, I noticed John's eyebrows raised and his countenance brightened. So when I got back on the phone with April, I asked what she had told him. She said that she told him Caden would be coming to see him next week. We were so pleased to see John's apparent excitement at the news that he would get to see Caden soon!

We all know how it goes in the waiting room…you wait. By 12:00 pm we were still waiting. It was not a big deal because John was resting and doing great, but as it got close to lunch, he woke up and started to vocalize. We all know John is disciplined about his eating habits, and he doesn't skip meals. He normally was fed six meals a day through his pegtube, and he knew that he was missing another one. Because of his toning and brain fevers, he needed at least 4,000 calories a day to keep him from losing weight. I began to talk to him and let him know that I was aware he was getting hungry, but because of the surgery he was just going to have to wait.

One of the nurses came in about that time to check on us. I mentioned that he was getting hungry, and the nurse said, "Well, John, then I'll be sure to eat more lunch just for you." As the nurse and I laughed, we noticed that John gave a little smile. God is doing a new thing! First, we saw raised eyebrows earlier that morning and now the smile!

The anesthesiologist came in and asked me how we would like to have John anesthetized. I could not believe he asked me that! I asked for a spinal because his trach had been out for over two weeks so I knew he couldn't use that. The anesthesiologist ruled that out because the muscles in John's back were so tight, he would not be able to do a spinal. I just said to him, "You need to ask the Lord what to do." We really didn't want to put him back to sleep because he had not been awake that long, and we were concerned about anesthesia putting him back under. The anesthesiologist said he would do what was best for John.

The surgery took about 2 1/2 hours, and when it was over, the urologist informed me that the procedure went very smooth and all was well. The anesthesiologist, also, came out and told me that God showed him what to do, and John had done great being intubated. The doctors indicated John should not have any more problems with bladder stones. About twenty minutes post surgery, John's eyes popped open! He woke up with no problems from the anesthesia. How awesome is our God! He is restoring John!

The evidence of things hoped for has started to come to realization. The therapists were moving forward with John and expecting more purposeful response from him. The sensory therapist pulled out some flash cards and asked John to point to certain things. John did it - not once, not twice, not three times, but four times!

Sensory therapy ended, and we headed back to John's room to get ready for physical therapy. April and Dalton arrived to join us. I said to April, "Let's have Dalton sit with John since John hasn't seen him in a couple of days." April sat Dalton in John's lap just as his physical therapist came in. The therapist and I watched to see how John responded with Dalton. John's arms and body were totally relaxed, and he didn't tense up at all with Dalton sitting with him. This was a big difference from the usual muscle tone we saw from him.

April said, "Why don't you give Dalton a kiss, John?" And John lowered his head and moved toward Dalton to kiss him. This was beyond believable!

Everyone at TIRR were used to seeing Dalton with April most days, but had not met Caden yet. April said, "I wasn't ready for Caden to see John the way he was still asleep and completely nonresponsive, so I had waited until John began opening his eyes. When I brought Caden to see his dad, it was very emotional because I felt so bad for Caden seeing him unable to speak or really move. The only thing Caden seemed to notice was the 'bobo' on daddy's nose — this was part of John's road rash that was taking forever to heal. So all in all, Caden did great, but I was still unsure if I had made the right choice."

The family stood strong. It was difficult having a family business to run and trying to continue to carry on the day-to-day operations without

John's guidance as CEO. Everyone's heart was in Houston with John, but the business had to keep going. The entire staff stepped up, pulled a little harder and pledged their commitment to the business, working longer hours and doing whatever it took. Jené, John's younger sister who works in the office, was now taking her eight-month-old son to work. Usually, I took care of little Garrison during the day, but now I was in Houston. John's right-hand-man, Erasmo, along with his wife, Maria, who is John's secretary, were invaluable in keeping things at work in balance. Maria, also, took care of all of John's insurance and medical bills, making endless phone calls and trying to make sense out of the paper chaos. Everyone's lives had been touched by this bump in the road.

God did a lot of reconnecting of old friends and loved ones, just like he was reconnecting John's brain pathways. A vendor for the company came to Houston to see John, and when she got there, he was sleeping. She prayed as he slept, and then John woke up, turned toward her and tears came to his eyes.

James came to Houston on the weekends, and John always responded well to him. This was just another miracle showing that John was there and coming forth in God's time. These were the biggest footprints the family had to hold on to, and we would not be moved.

• • •

KEYS TO WALKING OUT A MIRACLE:
1. Walk in the grace the Lord gives you one day at a time.
2. Dig into the Scriptures and keep fighting.

Miracle Testimony

Katie Bouchillon

I have been blessed with knowing the Keller family for about 2 years. As John's Occupational Therapist during his admission at TIRR, I saw first-hand the miracles of the Lord. John's story is a unique one, in that, this family never gave up hope and never faltered.

The first day I met John and his family, I was treating him in a very busy gym. He was sweating profusely due to sympathetic brainstorming and had significant hypertonicity throughout his body. He was dependent for all trunk and head control, had no movement in his body and was unable to communicate. He resisted any passive movement that was attempted, and he had to be transferred by a mechanical lift. During my career I have seen a lot of injuries, and I remember thinking that this was one of the worst.

I explained to the family that recovery is a very long road, and they had to stay strong, not only for John, but for each other. Little did I know that I was "preaching to the choir," so to speak? The family knew exactly the battle they were facing; they knew what they had to do; and they made it happen. They stood strong in their faith, continued to pray and pushed John to his limits every day. They made time for each other and found the time to minister to the other *families in the hospital. There was always an encouraging word to be said, no matter how good or bad of a day it was for John. Never did I see them discouraged or irresolute, as they put their faith in the Lord and knew without a doubt that John was going to be healed. From April's first words in the emergency room when she made the commitment that "John was going to be just fine" until the day he, against all odds, independently walked out of TIRR - their faith was never shaken.*

John's commitment to healing, and their commitment to John is what allowed him the opportunity to progress as he did. He was pushed every day by his family, his friends and all the people at TIRR that knew him. John always had someone there by his side - encouraging him and pushing him forward in his recovery. From the time John opened his eyes every morning until he went to bed every night, there was someone by his side and some higher power looking over him. That I do not question. That I could feel.

Encouraging words of hope and faith were spoken every day, and Mrs. Jan's infectious laughter would spread through the halls of TIRR. I remember the rumblings in the hallways the day John took his first steps, and the day he spoke his first words. I am not sure if there was a dry eye in the whole hospital. Every day was like this for John and his family.

There were definitely days when more progress was made than others, but that is how recovery works. There is no road map, no rules on how your brain will recover. The only rule, which the Keller's proved true, is to stand strong in your faith and never waiver. I have seen families collapse and I have seen families rise above, but I have never seen anything like the Keller family. They, as a family, were truly inspiring - not only to John and his healing - but to myself as a therapist, the doctors, and the other families that were sharing this experience with them. The faith and the optimism that the family brought to the hallways of TIRR allowed so many others to find hope and faith in the healing process.

With all this family was going through, they still found the time to minister to others and share their experiences of hope, healing and faith in the Lord. I do truly believe that all things happen for a reason, and I believe John's reason was to give others hope, faith and understanding. This family changed the lives of everyone they met. They prayed, offered words of encouragement and told others of their tribulations and triumphs throughout John's recovery. In this type of environment, support is crucial. That is what they did. During John's stay at TIRR, a sign on his door stated "Miracle in Progress" - I have never believed anything to be so true.

Chapter 13

Breakthroughs to Recovery

April Keller

The muscles in John's body were so stiff from toning and posturing, he would slide right out of the chair if not caught in time. His toes were pointed to a minus 37 degree angle. If you tried to bend them or help relax them, it felt like you were going to break him in half. Several things had been discussed, agreed upon and tried. It was decided that John would be tested for Intrathecal Baclofen (ITB) Treatment for Spasticity.

ITB is used to treat spasticity that is severe or moderately severe in most of the body — arms and legs, and often the trunk — which cannot be adequately treated with oral medications and Botox. Baclofen is a muscle-relaxing medicine and helps relieve muscle tension and toning. When administered orally, it makes the patient sleepy and interferes with their workouts. Another option was the Baclofen pump, which can be inserted into the walls of the abdomen, and releases medication continuously directly to the spine bypassing the blood stream. This route eliminated the side-effects experienced when given orally. There is no age limitation to ITB, although most people treated with it are four-years or older with Cerebral Palsy.[1]

We had heard of other patients that had this pump surgically placed in their abdomen with amazing results. At this point, John really needed something like this. His legs were not bending and his feet were pointing, his arms were getting stiffer, and he was just getting altogether tighter. I tried and tried to work and stretch him out during the day, but it wasn't enough. So we were ready for this Baclofen trial. The trial came and it failed. It was decided that John would not make a good candidate for the pump as it did not show enough improvement in his movements.

When I heard that the trial failed, at first, I think I was almost relieved. Truthfully, I was scared about it, because we had been told that once it was implanted most patients used it for life. I was thinking: *how could John have this pump in his stomach and wrestle with the boys or play football in the yard?* I was thinking long term because I wanted John to be able to play with his kids and have a normal life once again. John lived life to the fullest and wouldn't settle for any handicaps in life. I was trying to think how he would think. We prayed about it and believed God would show us what to do. But as the days continued and John's spasticity continued to worsen, we knew he could not go on the way he was.

The family requested a second test, using a larger dose of the medication, and this time, he passed the test. This one appeared to show some major improvements in his spasticity. When the pump is surgically implanted, the medication can be increased and decreased by the doctor as needed, plus the patient can receive a higher dose than the amount provided orally. So again, God was in control and showed us that John needed this pump for now. We just agreed that John would get better, and someday the pump would be able to be removed.

The next decision concerned replacing the missing piece of John's cranium that was removed to relieve the pressure on his brain at the time of the accident. It had been proven by doing so in other patients, a lot more progress, healing, and improvements occurred after replacement. The decision was made to replace the missing cranium and place a Baclofen pump in John's abdomen. To do so, however, would mean leaving TIRR and going to a new place. God would have to find that place for John.

During the first part of June, John had ups and downs. At times high blood pressure, elevated pulse and pain caused him to miss therapy sessions. Other days, he had some real breakthroughs and was alert and responding to everyone's commands, such as blinking, grabbing, squeezing or letting go of hands, and raising his eyebrows. In one sensory session, his therapist held up three foam shapes and told him that unless he moved her hand away, she was going to put the star on his head. John slowly reached up and pushed her hand away.

As they continued working, he seemed to want the towel in the therapist's lap. The therapist gave the towel to John, and he put the towel to his mouth and was able to wipe it, just as we had been coaching him to do. He was listening and remembering the command the therapists wanted to see all along. A few minutes later, the therapist tried to take the towel away, and he grabbed hold tighter and wouldn't let her take it. This was BIG!!! Everyone was impressed and encouraged. The family rejoiced that the Lord is reconnecting all the damaged or destroyed areas of John's brain.

The speech therapist expressed how great John was doing in her sessions as well. She said he was eager and tried hard to respond and do whatever he was asked to do.

Within a week, we were still in a holding pattern with John. He was having a bit of difficulty with an infection in his body and the pain it was causing. This caused him to revert back to toning and tensing up a lot, which was so hard on his body physically. Everyone was praying constantly over him that he would relax and be at peace. James said, "We are not moved by what we see, because we know greater is He that is in us than he that is in the world."

The other issue was where John was going to be moving to. The facility I had found notified me that they felt John was too "high needs" for their staffing level. What a disappointment this was. John's surgery to have the Baclofen pump inserted in his abdomen and the piece of cranium replaced in his skull was only three weeks away. TIRR was trying to assist us in finding a bed, but the facilities all said John's care level was more than they could handle. Finally, Jan placed a call to a facility where the administrator was married to a man from our hometown. A bed opened up and John moved to University Place Nursing Center on June 26, 2008.

It was such an emotional time leaving TIRR. We had connected with so many people. We had become friends and shared our hearts and our lives with them because we knew we were in good hands, but it was time to go. I cried when we left, but we were told there was a chance we could get John back in after he had some more time to heal.

• • •

Blog June 25, 2008:

God broke through and we are moving to the next place! University Place Nursing Center is about thirty minutes away from our current location, and the door is open for John to move there. They were very welcoming and kind when we spoke to them on the phone. Saying goodbye to everyone is not as easy as you think it would be. Every single person here at TIRR has been a huge blessing to us. But as Jan was saying her goodbyes to the nurses, therapists, techs, and patients she began to see miracles. One of the men we had prayed for back in the ICU at The Methodist Hospital is in a bed down the hall from John. He is leaving TIRR this week and doing very well. There is another patient that is now speaking. Another patient is bringing his finger to his nose. So we know our breakthrough is coming. John is getting ready to move forward in a mighty way. We can feel it in the atmosphere!

• • •

KEYS TO TALKING OUT A MIRACLE:

1. Consider all the options – short term and long term – when making decisions.
2. Let God order your steps to the next place you need to be.

Miracle Testimony

Marcie R. Roettger

W*hen I think of John, I am filled with many different emotions. I re-member his first and last days at TIRR like they were yesterday. His story is the one that I will never forget. As John's physical therapist, I had the op-portunity to watch him make gains that I had not experienced with any patient before - seeing him start out minimally conscious on day one of rehab to seeing him months later walking and talking as he started on his journey home from the hospital. John fought hard through so much on the days in between that to see his progress in the end seemed nothing less than miraculous.*

Early in his stay at TIRR, John and April went on a group outing to tour the football stadium. When they returned, one of the therapists said to me, "His wife isn't being very realistic. She got upset while we were there because she thinks when they go to future games that he'll be walking and not in a wheel-chair. They go to games frequently, and she can't imagine him going like this." Months later, when they went on another group outing to Target, John was able to walk with assistance; and when he checked out, he knew exactly how to work the credit card machine without missing a beat. A few months later, I remember his mother, Jan, came running down the hallway telling everyone that John had started talking! Amazing! I thought once again, John Keller is absolutely amazing!

From the very beginning, I knew John's family would not settle for less than getting back the John they knew. Their ability to stay positive was infectious to everyone around them. They did all they could for John and took the rest of us in like we were family. John and his family give me inspiration on so many levels. I hope the very best for him and look forward to seeing what great things are to come in his future.

Marcie R. Roettger, PT
Brain Injury & Stroke Program
TIRR/Memorial Hermann

Chapter 14

Moving Toward Victory

Jan Keller

U niversity Place Nursing Center is a skilled-nursing facility where mostly senior citizens came after having surgery or a stroke and were dismissed after further healing or rehabilitation. April felt uneasy in this new place.

• • •

April Keller

This was a huge shock for me. I passed several rooms with patients older than my grandparents. John was put in a room with an older gentleman who loved watching his news on TV with it blaring for all to hear. The room was tight with a few dressers for clothes and a small bathroom to share. It had no shower for John, no wheelchair, just a bed that was too short for his 6'5" frame.

As I got him settled, I went into the bathroom and cried. I don't believe they ever had a patient like John before. There was only one nurse for numerous patients, and no one seemed to have any idea what to do with John.

For me, it was a real unsettling feeling for sure. I only knew that God was somehow in control. It was not clear to me why He led us to this place, but I knew it had to get better and John was there for a reason.

• • •

Jan Keller

When the charge nurse came in and saw April with Dalton, she took action quickly to find John a private room. This gave April the privacy to nurse Dalton, and it was better because John liked his room cooler so they could keep the temperature at his liking. This nurse had a newborn of her own, and she loved on April and Dalton whenever she could.

The techs told us when they assessed John, they didn't know what to do for him. April and I told them we would be there to help because TIRR had taught us what to do and how to handle and care for John. He was still very stiff, with his legs literally straight out in front of him and transferring him was difficult to do alone, even with an electric lift.

I loved it because I was able to stay at night with John, and he rested better knowing someone was with him. I was impressed how the tech came in during the night and moved John on his side, and then switched his positioning again in another three hours.

Going to therapy meant going to a room full of patients in wheelchairs or lying on mats. The staff asked April what TIRR did, and she showed them how to do all the exercises with John that we did during his exercise class time. The therapists were very nice and wanted to help, but John was quite a challenge with his level of spasticity. So April took over and worked him out like she was taught at TIRR. They had trained us pretty well, and we were always involved.

April was upset one day when she came in to work John out in the corner of the gym, and someone had put an adult bib on John that resembled a towel with a circle cut out for his head and snapped in the back. She said, "John, you would absolutely hate this. You are wearing a bib, for crying out loud!" Thankfully he doesn't remember any of it. This was probably the hardest three months of John's recovery for her. As time moved along, the people that worked there were great cheerleaders for John and the family, and they loved April and the boys!

Now that John was in his new place and resting well, the task of scheduling the two surgeries was at hand. The first would be the replacement of his cranium, and then at the end of the month the Baclofen pump would be put into place.

The family agreed and began asking the Lord to work a mighty miracle in John's body during the replacement of his skull surgery, and for the Lord to use that to give John the breakthrough his body needed to get control of his muscles. It was our prayer that through this, his healing would excel, and there would be no need for the muscle-relaxer (Baclofen) pump.

James said, "I know God is bigger than the spasticity in John's muscles. He can work a miracle in this area, and we are asking for God to be John's physician so he won't need the pump."

My soul finds rest in God alone; my salvation comes from him.
He alone is my rock and my salvation; He is my fortress, I will
never be shaken.

Psalm 62:1-2 NIV

During the nights, when the techs came and turned John, it woke him. But when they told him to close his eyes and just go back to sleep, he did just that. They were surprised he did it. One of his techs used to work at TIRR, and she told us John was helping her more while she was getting him dressed. I was seeing John moving his left arm more as well.

The night nurse shared her testimony with me. She was saved after she lost her husband in Africa, and then she moved to the United States. Now she is married to a pastor. Praise the Lord for His ever present love! It is amazing how He is surrounding us. Honestly, it is so special because of the encouragement and confirmation of His promises it brings.

Then, a wonderful thing happened one morning! John woke up before me and started making noises to tell me he was awake! This was a first! Later that day, one of the vendors for the family business came by and brought John a "goodie basket." She was talking to John and began to cry. Then she noticed tears in John's eyes as well. The tech was there and saw his response. Everyone was moved and touched.

From such incidents, we were convinced John was aware of his surroundings and happenings. We kept praying for the Lord to continue healing the base of John's brain. We believe the Lord was building John a new foundation, a strong and firm foundation and drawing John out of the darkness and into His glorious light.

We had a meeting with the staff at University Place, and the staff expressed how impressed they were with the way April worked with John. We were then granted clearance to use the physical therapy room for John whenever we needed it. This was such a blessing to have that spacious area to work with John at any time.

John's tentative date for the cranium surgery was set for July 9, 2008, and later changed to July 15th. We were already starting to pray over that surgery and what the Lord wanted to do for John during that step. Also, we were praying for the balancing act of keeping the shunt working well. Some adjustments would have to be made after the cranial piece was replaced, and we wanted God to step in mightily to prevent any negative side effects! July is the seventh month of the year and the number "seven" in the Bible means *complete*. We were asking God to complete the healing process.

April and Dalton stayed with John, while the Keller family spent the Fourth of July weekend in New Braunfels, Texas at a family reunion. This was such a wonderful time together. As James and I, Caden, and Charles' kids - James, Tiara and Tatiana - headed back to Houston, we stopped for gas. In the parking lot of the gas station, James met a man, who was the Chapter Elder in Corpus Christi of Texas Bikers for Christ. He and James made an immediate connection, and they prayed right there in the convenience store for John's total healing. He promised to send out a prayer request so their prayer warriors could start praying: All 10,000 of them! That was just another God appointment!

Back at University Place Nursing Center later in the day, the Lord led James to cover and pray over the area of John's head that had the missing piece of skull. When he did that, John really responded to him and raised his eyebrows. He was very attentive to what James was praying, and the Spirit of the Lord came into John's room!

While we were at the family reunion, my sister gave me a CD with healing Scriptures on it. This was playing while James was praying over John. The Lord's presence was so sweet in that room, James began to weep.

About that time, I turned around and noticed the doctor and his resident had come in to do their rounds. I told them to come on in, and we could turn off the CD so they could do what they were there to do. The doctor replied, "No… just let them keep on." He was so touched and impressed by John's responsiveness that he wanted to see what all would happen. Later, the doctor said he really liked what he saw.

Later as James and I talked, we realized John had been awake almost all day. Aside from a few little cat naps here and there, he stayed awake the whole time. God was bringing him forward!

> *I waited patiently for the Lord, and he inclined unto me, and heard my cry. He brought me up also out of an horrible pit, out of the miry clay, and set my feet upon a rock, and established my goings. And he hath put a new song in my mouth, even praise unto our God; many shall see it, and fear, and shall trust in the Lord.*
>
> Psalm 40:1-3 KJV

On July 15, everything was in place for the cranium surgery. I was staying with John around the clock in the hospital before and after the surgery. God was moving on John every minute of every day, and we were seeing great things. We were all praying for the Lord to watch over John; for the doctors who were to operate on him; for the cranium piece to fit perfectly; for there to be no complications whatsoever; for John to wake up speedily after the surgery and sedation; for God to fill the operating room with a multitude of angels and guide the doctors in every decision.

John's surgery had been pushed back a little because the one in front of him had taken longer than expected, but by late afternoon, the doctor came out and said John did great and all went well! All of our prayers were answered.

Decisions were made to take him off the neuro-stimulants, and each day after that we saw improvements. John was more relaxed, in control, and responsive, even to the point of making sounds. It was really awesome to see!

John's right side had been extremely tense and stiff due to the muscle toning. So, the therapist in the hospital began working out his right arm, bending it and stretching it. That afternoon John bent it and moved his right arm twice! No one asked him to do it; it was the Lord building that connection and rewiring his brain to be aware and have control over that area of his body. Of course, we immediately laid hands on him and began to pray over every inch of his entire body. We began commanding each muscle, joint and tendon to receive its healing. It was wonderful to see the Lord minister healing to John's body and spirit.

July 17, 2008: The date was the seventeenth day of the seventh month. "Seven" means *complete* and "seventeen" means *victory*. James began declaring and decreeing "complete victory" over John that day! He said, "Today, John will have complete victory in Jesus' name! Victory over the toning! Victory over the high blood pressure and pulse! Victory over any pain! Victory in his healing! Amen!"

We were blessed by our nurse at the hospital when he told us that he saw John was doing a lot more than what the chart said he was capable of doing. We agreed, but it was a wonderful confirmation to hear! We had known all along that John was working hard to connect and respond to us even though the doctors were not acknowledging it. And now the nurse confirmed what we were seeing. He also told us we need to get the toning to stop and then John would really move forward. So, we started asking and commanding the toning to be gone from John's body in Jesus' name.

That night a new battle emerged. John was fighting high blood pressure and an elevated pulse most of the night. But by morning, it was finally under control and John was resting well.

The next day some good news came forth! The doctor said the CT scan looked good, and John would not have to wear his helmet anymore - no more 1920's style football helmet. We laughed because during this walk, a movie came out called "Leatherheads" so sometimes we called John that, or "Iron Man," which was the name of another popular movie at the time. It was really good to see John without the depression in his head and not wearing a helmet anymore. It made his head hot, and he really didn't like wearing it either. So this showed great progress.

James got excited and declared: "It's all about God! It's all to bring glory to His name! That is why we live, to bring His light into the world!"

Another good word came forth! John's nurse, who also has a son named Caden, said John's toning was not as bad as he had seen in other patients. He went on to say that those patients who have had the Baclofen pump put in, come back walking and talking to say "thank you" to the doctors and nurses who took care of them. Praise the Lord for that good word! We were believing God for His perfect timing and for directing our path! Oh, how wonderful that would be! To see John released from all that was holding him back.

James asked John if John knew who he was. John blinked his eyes, raised his eyebrows, and moved his left hand! That was such good confirmation that John was aware of everyone and who we are. We declared victory in Jesus!

> *Praise the Lord, all you nations; extol Him, all you peoples.*
> *For great is His love toward us, and the faithfulness of the Lord*
> *endures forever. Praise the Lord.*
>
> Psalm 117:1-2 NIV

John was sent back to University Place Nursing Center to await the surgery for the Baclofen pump. On Monday, July 21, very unexpectedly, John had a seizure while he was getting dressed. They worked all day running blood tests and such to try to find out what caused it but could never identify anything substantial. His sodium levels came back normal, so it was not caused by an electrolyte imbalance. However, the positive side to this was that this meant that those brain neurons were not dead – they were just confused. Now we started praising the Lord for the living, confused neurons and commanding them to get into order and have direction. We commanded the confusion and seizures to cease in Jesus' name.

And with that John did not have any more seizures. Everyone really felt it was a one-time thing, and there was nothing new going on. But the family continued to follow the doctor's advice concerning his recommendation, as a preventative measure, to put John on an anti-seizure medicine each morning and night.

The next day was a really big breakthrough! John's arms didn't tone at all, and because of the increased looseness, he got to use the arm bike during his workout! He tolerated it for a long time, using both arms. An arm bike wheel is essentially a table-top bicycle wheel with bike pedals, but you use your hands to pedal the wheel. This was a big accomplishment! It was good for John to be able to do that kind of workout to bring more healing to his brain. He, also, worked out on his stomach, which allowed him to stretch out his chest muscles better. During all of this, his pulse stayed in the 60s. We prayed Psalm 91 over John.

Another tremendous achievement for John was that he wiggled his toes on command. To see his toes move at all was an unexpected and rare event. Now for him to do it when asked was definitely worthy of a "Praise the Lord!"

We found out that the Baclofen pump could not be implanted into John yet, because the doctor said it was too soon after his cranium surgery.

So we said to the Lord, "Thank you for knowing more than we do! We will be patient, rest, and have faith in You." It had been our prayer from the beginning that the Lord would heal John, and the Baclofen pump would not be necessary at all. Now we just kept praying for that healing to come.

He had the staples taken out from his cranium surgery and did well all through the night. John was fitted with some new hand and foot splints. This was to help prevent anymore loss of range of motion. He was getting his workouts every day. His brother Charles was in town during the week, and it was a blessing to have his help. April and Charles gave John some good workouts, including getting John back onto the arm bike.

During that time, I went to lunch with two close friends in the Houston area. Our waitress was such a sweet girl so I started talking to her. She was a Christian and had just graduated from Texas Bible Institute in Columbus, Texas. That is where James and I took our youth to camp for many years. Our son, Charles' kids were going to camp there the next week, and James is on the Board of Regents for the Camp.

During that same lunch, a lady walked by the table and stopped. She looked at me and said, "I know you from somewhere." It took us a few moments to realize we had been on a business cruise together a few years back. She and her husband had just moved to Houston from New Jersey. Isn't our God just mind blowing? Honestly, as if one connection wasn't enough for one day. He sent two people across my path just to drive it home that He sees the very location we are at and connections are happening.

God was just confirming to us that He sees us and knows right where we are. He knows where you are, too. Just call out to Him. Ask Him to connect you with people who will help hold you up and pray with you through difficult times. Everything you are going through matters to Him because He loves you. He loves you so much He gave His life for you. What a mighty God we serve!

• • •

KEYS TO WALKING OUT A MIRACLE:
1. Be at peace wherever He leads you.
2. Remember: God is bigger than any obstacles that try to block your path.
3. Ask God to connect you with people who will help hold you up and pray you through difficult times.

Testimony 14

Miracle Testimony

Jimmy Villanueva

My name is Jimmy Villanueva. My wife, Lizzy, and I currently reside in Sugar Land, TX where I work as a worship pastor of a local church. I used to be the youth group worship leader at Abundant Grace Community Church and worked alongside James, Jan and their family for many years.

When the news hit about John, we were shocked but immediately began praying because we knew that nothing is impossible for our Great GOD! When John was moved to Houston, we visited him frequently. Usually I brought my guitar and just played for him. We worshiped together in his room! I say "we," because I know John was listening and worshipping along with me. Seeing the progress John was making each visit, was nothing short of a miracle!

My wife and I were happy to be there with him and the family as he was being restored. We often went to Luby's with Jan and just talked about the goodness of God! It was never negative. Every conversation I had with her was full of hope! Wow, to have a faith like that is something we all need. It was, also, a blessing to hang out with the kids when April needed some help. April was so strong during it all! She has been such example of what it means to live out your marriage vows. In sickness and in health she was there!

I was so encouraged when I talked to James. I remember a conversation I had with him over the phone toward the one year mark. I asked him what he learned through all this. With tears he said, "God is real, Jimmy." We cried and prayed together. I can say honestly with my whole heart, I'm a better man because of James and conversations like that!

John, you have touched thousands of lives! We love you and stand with you, proclaiming the goodness of GOD! The best is yet to come!

Chapter 15

New Beginnings

James Keller

August dawned with great hope and expectation. The number "8" in Hebrew means *new beginnings*, and we were definitely ready for something new to start happening in John's recovery. A prophetic word had come forth that in the first week of August, John would do three new things. The first thing occurred when John brought his eyes to midline, was focused and tracked well. Since he was on some pretty strong medications, this was especially significant.

• • •

April Keller

We started to work on John's focusing ability. Up until this point, John was looking like a deer in headlights with a blank look in his eyes and very little tracking of objects or people. But anyone who knew John could agree that John never met a mirror he didn't like…so that is exactly where we started. We put him in front of a mirror for every exercise. By doing this, we got him to actually focus on looking at himself in the mirror and could sometimes get him to look at Dalton or me. This was a huge step that took lots of effort on his part and lots of coaxing on our part. But I pushed John everyday to help him get better. I knew God was going to do it, but I didn't want any of the blame to fall on me because I didn't do my part. So, as John will tell you, my nickname became and still is, "Mrs. Pushy!

• • •

James Keller

The second new thing was even bigger! Another patient came into the physical therapy room to work out all decked out in UT (University of Texas) pajamas, house shoes, etc. UT and Texas A&M have a long-standing rivalry between the two schools. Of course, everyone at University Place Nursing Center knew John is an Aggie graduate, and they started saying, "John, are you going to let him get away with that? Why don't you give him a Gig 'Em Aggies? Come on, John, you can do it!" And John did it! He gave a "two thumbs up," Gig 'Em Aggies sign! Twice! It took him a while but he did it. Go Aggies!

The third new thing came later in the week. Saturday morning when Jan was working John out, he reached up and touched his chin! Jan was totally surprised, but she didn't stop there. She asked him to take his finger and touch his nose. He was obedient and did it! Jan called out to the other therapists in the room to make sure everyone saw it. All the therapists and patients cheered and clapped for John. They thought it was just wonderful!

The Lord is good. A stronghold in the day of trouble; and He knows those who trust in Him.

Nahum 1:7 NAS

John had more surprises in store for Jan that day. As she was getting him dressed and ready for the day, she was leaning over him brushing his teeth. She felt something on the back of her head and turned to see what it was. John's right hand was touching the back of her head. He had not moved the right side of his body voluntarily at all until now. Again, we praised the Lord for the great and mighty things He was doing and was yet to do.

A fun thing then happened when Jan was taking John outside to get some afternoon sun. She put John's sunglasses on him when they left his room. Before they had gotten outside, John had taken them off, folded them and put them in his lap! Everyone was amazed that John could do this!

He reached down from on high and took hold of me; he drew me out of deep waters. He rescued me from my powerful enemy, from my foes, who were too strong for me. They confronted me in the day of my disaster, but the Lord was my support. He brought me out into a spacious place; he rescued me because he delighted in me.

Psalm 18:16-19 NIV

In August, Jan and April started doing a two-week-on, two-week-off rotation with John in order to bring some sense of routine and quality time at home for both of them. April and the boys were in Houston the first two weeks of the month and her parents continued to be with her during the week to help with the boys. Later in the fall, April started taking the boys to a nearby daycare during the week. Jan covered the last two weeks of the month.

When Jan returned after her first two-week absence, she was really impressed with how good John looked and how much he was doing. His skin and mouth looked great. He responded immediately when she came in and moved his mouth trying to make noises. Then he moved his right arm and tried to give her a hug. She was excited to be back and real encouraged with seeing such a big difference.

Jan's college roommate, Suzanne, had never met John, but during her visit, she could tell how special he was. Suzanne spoke life to John's body and began telling him to confess with his mind what the Lord could do for him. They had been listening to a CD of a man sharing his testimony of how he had been healed. I shared with her all of the Scriptures I had put on a CD for John's healing.

It was time to meet with the doctor from TIRR for John's re-evaluation. We had requested permission for John to be re-admitted to TIRR after he had the Baclofen pump placed. John was, also, scheduled to have more Botox injected into his muscles to help with the toning and tension. While getting John ready for his Botox appointment, he reached up his right hand as if to try to shake Jan's hand. She was really moved by that, acknowledged it, and then told John, "When we get to the doctor's office this afternoon, I want you to show him what you can do. John, I want you to reach up and shake his hand, OK?"

In the ambulance ride to the doctor's office, the EMS personnel were listening to Christian music, so Jan began to share John's testimony. Once they were at the doctor's office, Jan was talking to the doctor when she noticed out of the corner of her eye that John was raising his right hand up. She stopped and told the doctor, "See? I asked John earlier this morning if he would shake your hand when we came to meet with you. And look he is doing it. He wants to shake your hand."

The doctor was very impressed, in fact, so impressed that he got on the phone with the insurance company and demanded that they cover the cost of the Botox treatment! The doctor, also, told Jan a testimony of a man in a similar situation to John's. The doctors all diagnosed him as being in a "persistent vegetative state," but the family knew and believed otherwise. So, they pushed for him to receive the Baclofen pump, and after it was inserted, the man began to move his arms and learned to talk again. This was confirmation for us to believe great things were in store for John's future.

> *They are abundantly satisfied with the fullness of Your house,*
> *and You give them drink from the river of Your pleasures. For*
> *with You is the fountain of life; in Your light we see light.*
> Psalm 36:8-9 KJV

A gentleman in the room next to John's at University Place was fighting cancer and had lost his wife some years ago. His daughter came to visit him, but she was battling a serious illness as well. One day when their paths crossed, she shared with Jan that she had begun praying for "J. Keller" from the first time she visited her father. She said she smelled a sweet aroma coming from his room every time she walked by it. We knew it was the fragrance of the Holy Spirit, and she was sensing the Lord's presence in John's room.

So, the Lord allowed our family to be connected to her, and we began praying for them, just as they were praying for John. We still hear from this woman. She continues to visit her dad who has had more surgeries. She believes she is healed today because of our prayers.

When I came into town to be with John, I worked him out hard. I asked John to lift his legs - five times, up and down - and he did it. The charge nurse came to John's room before leaving to say good night, and she asked John to raise his right arm for her, and he did it. He was working so hard to show everyone that he was getting better and better every day!

The long awaited day of August 26, 2008 arrived for John's surgery to implant the Baclofen pump. It was, also, John and April's 8th wedding anniversary, but this was the only date available for the surgery to be done. The people at the plant in Puerto Rico that distributes the pump were on strike, and this was the last day any pumps would be available for use until the strike was settled. God's timing is always perfect!

• • •

Blog August 26, 2008:
Just to give you a little bit of an update. John and Jan went to the hospital via ambulance around 10:00 am. His surgery will begin sometime around 4:30 pm and will last 4 hours. He will be in ICU for a little while and from there he will

go back to University Place Nursing Center. Thank you for your prayers!

7:30 pm: John is out of surgery and in recovery. He did very well with no complications. He really did great all day today and didn't have any pain medication at all until surgery. Praise the Lord! Now the level of medication to be administered for the pump will be regulated by the doctors at TIRR. He will be getting low doses for the next few days, and then he has an appointment to see a TIRR doctor. The doctor will adjust the medication until he finds what benefits John best. We look forward to the next weeks as we know the Lord is going to bring about great things for John.

• • •

The day after the surgery at The Methodist Hospital, John spent most of the day in bed and got a lot of good rest. As the resident came by to check on John, he asked John to raise two fingers on his left hand. Praise the Lord, John did exactly what was asked! Then the hospital caseworker stopped by to see John, and he did exactly what she asked of him too!

Jan, who had learned to text from her cell phone through this journey, sent out a text saying, "The staff was so excited to see John. They can really see improvement, even in his neck. It is such a blessing to see him moving forward! Glory to God!"

Just as the month of August started out with new beginnings, so it closed with yet more exciting new beginnings for John's miraculous healing. Here's an example of what was in store as recorded in Jan's journal:

"Over the weeks of going back to TIRR via ambulance transports, the doctor's orders started with 150 cc of Baclofen and ended up with 220 cc of Baclofen dispensed directly into his spinal cord to release the muscle relaxer into his legs. At the time of John's surgery, his legs were straight out in front of him when sitting in his wheelchair. He was very stiff. Later in September, he was sitting in the wheelchair with his knees bent and his feet on the foot-rests of the wheelchair!"

God was moving mightily on John's behalf, and His promises were being fulfilled at a more rapid pace. The replacement of the piece of his cranium and the insertion of the Baclofen pump were making a huge difference in his ability to move his limbs and in many of his cognitive functions. God continued to lead us each step of the way toward John's healing and full recovery.

• • •

KEYS TO WALKING OUT A MIRACLE:
1. Watch for new things to start happening.
2. Rejoice when surprises come your way.
3. Record or journal the signs or miracles no matter how small they may be.
4. Pray in healing and miracles for others that cross your path.

John at 5 years old.

John on his motorbike
at 7 years old.

John, Charles, Jene and Jennifer.

John's Graduation from
Texas A&M, 1998.

John and April on their engagement, Spring of 2000.

John, April and Caden, Spring of 2006.

Caden on John's Bike, Summer 2007.

John working on his bike, 2007.

Jan & James Keller.

John and Aggie before the accident.

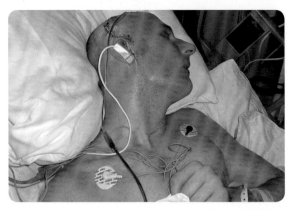

John after cranium replacement, July of 2008.

Dalton and Caden visiting Daddy, August of 2008.

John working on the hand bike, September of 2008.

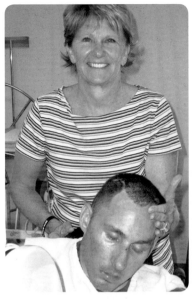

Jan and John going to therapy,
September of 2008.

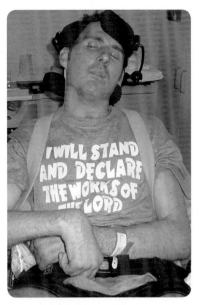

John wearing his Psalm 118 shirt,
October of 2008.

April and John attending his
TIRR farewell party,
January of 2009.

John walking out of TIRR,
going home, Jan 29, 2009.

April, John, Caden and Dalton in the golf cart, February of 2009.

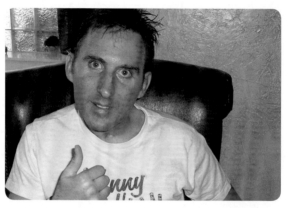

John giving the Aggie thumbs up on being home, February of 2009.

John relaxing with Caden and Dalton, February of 2009.

April, John, Caden, Dalton on
vacation, May of 2009.

John speaking to students at a
Physical Therapist Assistant Program
about TBI, November of 2009.

John and Michael at a Speech
Therapists' Convention,
November of 2009.

John at the new Dallas Cowboys
stadium, December of 2009.

Family Christmas, December of 2009.

John, January of 2010.

Miracle Testimony

Melissa Chase

I have known John Keller since he was 6 years old and babysat for him. I have kept up with his family through the years. When Jan called to tell me about John's accident, I began to pray for God to restore John and protect him. I, also, asked God to use me to minister and encourage John's family. I drove to McAllen a few days after the accident and the seriousness of his condition really sunk in. The Keller's and those standing with them had ongoing prayer in the waiting room not only for John but, also, for the other patients and families in the ICU.

When John was transferred to Houston, I was able to go there some week-ends to help with John's care and to be with Jan. After we tucked John in for the night, she and I would go to a movie and dinner. Everywhere we went, God put people in our path to share about what God was doing in John's life and the miracle that was taking place at TIRR. Jan never failed to reach out to others and to encourage them. What a blessing it was to watch and learn how to praise the Lord in all circumstances.

When I heard that John was talking, I rushed down to hospital! He was talking and making phone calls! When he said my name, I was in tears. At that *point I knew how real God is and that He is capable of doing more then we can ever ask or hope for. I have always considered it a privilege to know the Keller family. They have truly shown me Jesus as they walked through this journey. Watching John's recovery has made me confident in Christ, knowing that He alone is faithful, sovereign and trustworthy!*

We don't get to pick the lessons God teaches us, but I know He is God, and He walks with us and sometimes carries us through it all!

Chapter 16

A Miracle in Progress

James Keller

After the placement of the Baclofen pump, John returned to University Place Nursing Center. He seemed to be drowsy and sleepy at first, but there was a major difference in all that John was now able to do. Jan talked to another mother whose daughter had the Baclofen pump put in, and she said her daughter slept a lot right after the pump was placed. We learned that the fatigue was attributed to how worn out John's body was due to the tenseness and toning he had been experiencing for such a long period of time.

A few days later, John had an appointment with the doctor at TIRR to evaluate the medication level of the Baclofen pump. While waiting for the ambulance to take them back to University Place Nursing Center, John raised his right arm again and touched his hand to his chin. Jan praised him and said, "Way to go, John. You touched your chin. Good job!" Then he partially opened his fingers and rubbed his nose. She was so excited to see that voluntary movement, it brought tears to her eyes, and again she praised John enthusiastically.

Although John's movements were slow and sometimes small; we had eyes to see all that the Lord was doing to heal, reconnect, restore and renew John's brain and body. Because of the prayers of so many people, John stayed healthy and had no complications. We declared that in Jesus' name, he would not have sickness or complications in the future.

> *And we can be confident that He will listen to us whenever we*
> *ask Him for anything in line with His will. And if we know*
> *He is listening when we make our requests, we can be sure that*
> *He will give us what we ask for.*
>
> I John 5:14-15 NLT

A series of "miracles" began to happen all within a short time. In the middle of the night, one of the techs posted a sign above John's bed that said, "John Keller - Miracle in Progress." When I heard about this the next morning, I said, "And we say Hallelujah to that! Because we know the presence of the Lord is residing there in the room with John, healing him and restoring him…touching him and changing him!"

That is one of the great things about where John was. The people believed with us and prayed over him, laying hands on him continually! Our corporate faith was moving this mountain. We continued to lift up the Lord's name and give Him all the glory, because without Him we are nothing!

The next "miracle" came in the form of a phone call, and it was just another testimony of God putting people in our path to confirm His promise! Jan made a call to a utility company, and the lady that answered the phone was named "Miracle." So she shared the testimony of where we were walking and having ears to hear!

The third "miracle" was a new tech that arrived to take care of John whose name was "Milagro," which in Spanish, means *miracle*. I exclaimed, "What a faithful God we serve! Faithful to His word! Even in the small things, because He cares for us. Our faithful God is showing us great and wonderful things through John."

Three times the Lord had spoken MIRACLE. Once with the sign above John from one of his techs, Miracle answered the phone when Jan called the utility company, and now Miracle showed up at University Place Nursing Center. We were listening and in agreement that we were hearing the Lord right in the midst of us.

• • •

Blog September 4, 2008:
John worked out by using his arms to peddle on the arm bike. What some of you might not know is that his right wrist was completely drawn in and his arm was board straight and stiff a lot of the time. This had to be incredibly painful and uncomfortable for him. (Just so you can understand what I mean by his wrist being drawn in: hold your arm out straight in front of you, make a fist, and bend your wrist so your fist is pointing straight down to the ground.) But now, there is such a difference, and his wrist is much, much looser. The

Lord has proven faithful and we stand in awe of all that He has already done. But we also know He is not finished yet!

• • •

Surprises! Surprises! Surprises! April took Caden to see John. While Caden was eating his lunch, April made the comment to him to eat all his food so he could get muscles like his daddy. Unprompted, John raised up his right arm to show off his muscles to Caden! This meant that John was listening to their conversation!

More surprises! John was getting his shower, and the nurse accidentally got water in his eyes. She told him she was sorry and acknowledged that he probably didn't like it. Well, he just reached over, grabbed the towel, and brought it up to his eyes. Big-Big-Big!

When April was with him a little bit later, he was very awake, alert, and his eyes were looking straight ahead. April told him how good that was. Then she asked John to do several things: "Lift your right leg" - John did it. "Lift your left arm" - John did it. Each time she asked for something he did it. Then she had some colored cones, and she asked him to find the yellow cone. He grabbed it with his right hand. She asked him to find another color, and he again grabbed the correct cone with his right hand.

About this time, Jan received this encouraging word via a text message from the radiology tech from TIRR who had continued to pray for John and the family: "Good morning all! God is doing great things in your lives! Prepare yourself for a move of God. Don't entertain doubt. Press and fight your way to the end! You are almost there! And He is waiting at the finish line to reward you!"

The Scripture that spoke to us as being confirmation of this word came from Jeremiah 18:1-5 NIV:

> *This is the word that came to Jeremiah from the Lord: "Go down to the potter's house, and there I will give you my message." So I went down to the potter's house, and I saw him working at the wheel. But the pot he was shaping from the clay was marred in his hands; so the potter formed it into another pot, shaping it as seemed best to him. Then the word of the Lord came to me: "O house of Israel, can I not do with you as this potter does?" declares the Lord. "Like clay in the hand of the potter, so are you in my hand, O house of Israel.*

As John was leaping forward and making excellent progress, a storm in the Gulf of Mexico had formed and Hurricane Ike was heading straight for Houston. All non-essential people were being evacuated from the area, which meant that John would have to weather the hurricane alone at University Place. All family members were sent home to McAllen.

By September 15, 2008 it had been two days since Hurricane Ike made landfall, and John was doing well. One of our family business vendors went to check up on him that weekend in the middle of the hurricane. What a blessing! She conveyed that he was doing just fine. She let him know what was going on concerning the hurricane and that his family would be back as soon as the airports opened back up. Then she asked him to squeeze her hand if he understood all she was telling him, and he did!

While the facility had been operating on generator power, his room had not been as cool as he liked it. However, the therapists located a battery-powered fan during the power outage and decided to use it for John. The Lord has continually blessed John with such grace and favor. Everyone took exceptional care of him.

Jan was able to get back to Houston on September 16th and saw, first-hand, the effects of the wind and the strength of Ike. Trees were down everywhere and long lines were prevalent at the gas stations. The apartment was without power so she stayed with John because University Place Nursing Center finally had its power back on.

John was up in his chair when Jan got there, and he was completely relaxed. His eyes were midline - looking straight ahead and not off to the left - most of the day, and he was awake a lot of the time, too. When Jan arrived, he reached up to her as she hugged him, and she felt like John was trying to hug her back.

We know that the Lord watched over him perfecting all that He is doing in John. Because he had been in bed for several days, we asked everyone to pray that this time would prove to be a good time of rest and even more healing. We continued to wait for the medication level administered by the Baclofen pump to stabilize so that John might be eligible for re-admission to TIRR. Our trust was totally on the Lord, believing that John would not lack any good thing in the days ahead as this promise says:

Oh, taste and see that the LORD is good; blessed is the man who trusts in Him! Oh, fear the LORD, you His saints! There is no want to those who fear Him. The young lions lack and suffer hunger; but those who seek the LORD shall not lack any good thing.

Psalm 34:8-10 NIV

• • •

KEYS TO WALKING OUT A MIRACLE:

1. Keep your eyes on the small miracles to build your faith.
2. Don't entertain doubt. Press and fight your way to the end!

Miracle Testimony

Maria Mendez
Rosa Pallais

When April called Erasmo (my husband) to tell him that John had been in an accident, we immediately got in the car and started driving towards the hospital. Erasmo had been talking to John about going to the rodeo with him, laughing about how he would follow him "on" his F250 truck. John kept insisting Erasmo should ride with him on his bike, but Erasmo just wouldn't do it. So, we knew John was on his bike. As we left our house, not even a minute later, we came upon what appeared to be John's accident. We knew he was driving north on 10*th* but we couldn't understand why the bike was 5 lanes down all the way on the southbound lane next to the curb...

I just remember calling April who was at home waiting for her mom and saying, "What are you doing? Why aren't you on your way? You need to get there ASAP. It doesn't look good." I didn't tell her what we saw, of course, just to get to the hospital fast!

We got to the hospital and found James, Jan and April at the Emergency Room. We just started praying and that is when James told us the doctors had put John into an induced coma, and the accident was very serious.

Some people talk-the-talk, but the Keller's walk-the-walk. This is where the "walk-the-walk" started…

From that day forward, we prayed and prayed and prayed, but in a different way than how I was used to praying. Someone would quote a verse from the Bible, and it was like that verse was given to us to show us exactly what was happening with John and how to pray effectively. The prayers were always positive, thanking God for healing that was yet to be seen. The prayers were offered with so much faith that it was almost unreal to me. I was overwhelmed - in a good way - with the amount of faith these people had. There was never any doubt about what was going to happen: John will be healed, he will be just fine!

Working in the office for the Keller's, we have prayed for anyone that needed prayer. I have always loved the way they all pray - James and Jan and their kids. But seeing what I saw from day one of the accident to this day has been hugely different. Being able to pray positively, continually thanking God for what He has yet to do was not something I had ever seen.

My prayer life has changed tremendously. My faith has increased to levels that I didn't know existed. I have learned to pray in a different way and to be patient. Through all of this, we began to realize that God is in charge of our every move, but we have to wait until it's His right time for the answers to come. He can truly bless us with a wonderful life if we let Him. I have learned to listen more and pray and pray and pray until something happens. God speaks to you if you listen. Once His timing is where it needs to be, and you are where you need to be, He will unleash all his blessings.

John Keller is healed and more healing is still coming, but He has sent John back as a better man, a better husband and father, a better son, a better brother and a better friend. God always knows what He is doing, and we don't have the right to question Him in the decisions He makes. I can truly say that I'm glad God decided to give John back to all of us, because He has shown us how His mercy and power work for us even when the odds look impossible. Our lives have been forever changed!

● ● ●

Rosa Pallais

F*aith has been reflected on John Keller's testimony of life. It shows me one more time that prayer is powerful; that it's the best gift Jesus left us; and if we all are united in one petition, it has more strength.*

When my faith flickers, immediately this great example comes to my mind, of the Keller's - a family of Prayer and Faith.

After being touched and healed this way, it's impossible for John to keep quiet!! Everyone wants to shout to the world about God's great love. It's like in Jesus' time, when He told those He healed to keep quiet, but they couldn't remain silent!!! He wants us healed, full of life in the Holy Spirit, and to tell everyone the Good News just as John is doing.

Chapter 17

One More Hurdle To Go

Jan Keller

October began with one more hurdle for John to go over in his road to recovery. He was scheduled for surgery to relieve the tension on his legs and toes by cutting and lengthening the muscle tendons. This surgery would give John back the range of motion that was lost due to his posturing and toning for so long. He would have to wear casts for about 4-to-6 weeks after surgery. Once again, we were blessed to be in God's perfect timing. The surgeon was going on vacation, but he was able to see John and do the surgery before he left.

After the coma, we hated to have him go under anesthesia again, so we doubled up on prayer. When John came out of this surgery, for some reason, he had trouble waking up. As we were trying to arouse him, April called on the telephone and had 2½-year-old Caden talk to John. Caden had been praying for his daddy to wake up, so he started yelling to John over the phone, "Daddy, wake up! Daddy, wake up!" John's eyes started to blink, and he woke up!

After the tendon lengthening surgery and putting the casts on his legs and feet, the doctor wanted John to be put in the standing frame during therapy as soon as possible. This meant he would be standing up and getting ready to walk! The day after surgery he had already been up in his chair and outside in the morning. He watched his videos, looked at pictures on the computer of Caden and April at the ranch playing with Pop (James) and his cousin, Garrison, and visiting all the animals. It was so awesome to see how much God was doing for and through John.

We pulled out a poster with family member's names written on it and asked John to find Jennifer's name. He was looking at the names and found it with his eyes. Then we moved on to finding "Mom" in the list of names, and we asked him to point at it. He took his right hand and touched the board where "Mom" was written. We just cried and praised the Lord! We proclaimed over John that God was reconnecting and re-establishing him.

One of the most exciting answers to prayer came when we were notified that John was approved for re-admission to TIRR. John received such cutting-edge, aggressive therapy at TIRR the first time, we were very eager to see how the Lord was going to bring him forward now. We began praying for the therapists that would be working with him to be led by the Spirit and know just what John needed to draw out of him more communication, movement and healing.

We were in John's room at University Place Nursing Center, when a lady walked into the room and said, "Hi there. I have to tell you, I have never done this before." We knew the Lord had sent her, and she was being obedient to His voice. She proceeded to tell us when she had seen John in his room and began praying for him.

When she saw him take off his glasses and fold them while he was in the therapy room, it blew her away. She asked around to find out what his name was, searched on the Internet and found the blog. At this point, tears were running down our faces.

She went on to say that while she was praying for John, she had a vision of him sitting up in bed, and he began talking! We shouted, "Thank you Father, for sending her to us, just to confirm again that you are the God who sees. You are working all things together for John's good, and we praise Your name for everything! John Keller is healed in Jesus' name!"

This was so awesome! She mentioned how she felt the Lord tugging at her to come into his room to share with us. We were so thankful for her hearing heart and obedience.

When April was with John in therapy, she had him hold a marker to see if he could write. At first, he just held the marker and moved it around a little. Although, he hadn't written words yet, we knew it would not be long. His fine motor skills were coming back slowly but surely. He, also, performed the task of taking nuts and putting them onto small screws. When a nut fell into his lap, he reached down, picked it up, and then put it on the screw! This was incredible!

On October 8th TIRR notified us that they had a bed for John. This was the 8th day ("eight" means *new beginning*) of the tenth month October ("ten" means *testimony*). Hallelujah! Another door was opened by God for a new beginning for John and a testimony of God's goodness.

• • •

April Keller

John's second phase at TIRR began, and it felt like we were going back home. It was such a relief to know we were returning to the best rehab place for John and where we felt like family. I had kept in touch with John's doctor and therapists at TIRR, all along, with questions and concerns we had, and they were always available to help.

• • •

James Keller

John got settled in at TIRR and the same tech that worked with him the first time had asked if he could be assigned to her caseload. What a blessing it was to have such grace and favor! God orchestrated every move. John had appointments to be assessed by all of the therapies. We were eager to see how aggressive his new treatment plan would be.

One fun, positive thing happened. The physical therapist put a skateboard under John's right foot, and he knew instinctively to push it back and forth. We are confident that God is bringing forth more and more healing in John's brain. They are going to recast his feet in order to get a complete 90 percent range of motion.

Then on October 12th John was diagnosed with pneumonia and had to be moved back to The Methodist Hospital for x-rays and tests. He had to stay in intermediate care in the hospital until all the tests came back. We continued to pray that the Lord would quicken and strengthen John's ability to swallow. This would resolve the problems with aspirating saliva into his lungs that so easily turns into pneumonia.

John was discharged to return to TIRR on the evening of October 14th. We were excited to learn he was going back into room 310 – the Miracle Room – where he started the first time he was there. This was an answer to prayer since the nurses and techs on that floor all cared for John and were such a blessing. God's provision and timing were perfect!

A close family friend summed it up when she said, "I love when God doesn't just answer the big prayer but throws in little extras to let us know just how much He cares about us." April added, "So, a little bump in the road for all of us to get back to the place God intended was okay with me."

John settled in at TIRR again, and it was back to business. During his speech therapy session, April and the therapist decided to use "yes" and "no" questions and asked him to point to the answers. They asked a series of questions, and he pointed to every answer correctly. Are you a father? "Yes." Do you have boys? "Yes." Do you have girls? "No." Is April your sister? "No." Then they asked him to point to himself, Caden, and April in pictures, and he did that too.

. . .

April Keller

After quickly re-acquainting with the therapists and being introduced to a new young and positive occupational therapist, everyone was so happy to see us back. John was getting some results from the pump and his muscles were beginning to loosen up. He had begun moving his arms a lot more and his legs were not as stiff. Much of the initial time during therapy at TIRR was spent trying to find the right fit of a wheelchair for John to move around in, and John continued to improve and get looser every day, which made this task challenging.

One of the first things I tried to do with John now that he was back at TIRR, was to get him to write. Just before we had left University Place Nursing Center, I had him scribble on paper to start refining his writing skills. I felt it was time to pursue this further. One afternoon while we were outside enjoying the day, I gave him the paper and pen and said, "Let's try and write. Can you write Hi?" When he did it, I was blown away and called to tell Jan what he did. I even took a picture on my phone and sent it to James and Jan.

I wheeled John upstairs and then started telling everyone! I found our nurse, and asked John to write "hi" for him. John was able to do it even being careful to dot the "i." But the best part was that his nurse could read it. This meant that it wasn't just my eyes wanting to see the word, it was for real! Then we worked on "Hi Mom" and every day more and more words. We asked him to write his name and birthday, my name, and the kid's names…so many more things, and he knew all of them without us having to spell the words. Now we had confirmation that John was really there and understood! Praise God, he is in there!

Of course, lots more questions were to come and thus began our written communication for everything. We asked him if certain parts of his body hurt, or if he was tired, anything to give us an indication of how he was feeling. This was so awesome to communicate with him. However, there were many times when we couldn't understand what he was writing. We would ask him over and over again to rewrite it. Sometimes, we even had others look at it, and finally he would just underline what he wrote as if to say, "GET IT PLEASE!"

Charles called and talked to him one evening. I asked John if he was talking to his cousin. John didn't respond. Then I asked if he was talking to his brother, and he gave me a thumbs-up signal. John was communicating!

> *But without faith it is impossible to please Him, for he who comes to God must believe that He is, and that He is a rewarder of those who diligently seek Him.*
>
> Hebrews 11:6 NAS

• • •

Jan Keller

John was put in the standing frame during therapy, and they were stretching his neck almost daily. He could now be transferred from his bed to his chair without the use of the lift. A big answer to prayer – he passed his swallowing test and swallowed like a pro for his speech therapist.

The last week of October for John was miraculous. The Lord has been building new paths and connections in John's brain, and we stand in awe of what God is doing. John's doctor came in and notified us that he has been approved to stay at TIRR for six more weeks. This is such a gift from God. John was still writing some words and names, although sometimes he did not seem very interested in doing it. His left leg had begun to show signs of reconnection! He pushed the skate board back and forth with both feet when asked to do so. He supported his own weight and rested his elbows on his knees, while sitting down during occupational therapy.

James came in over the weekend and was so excited to see John peddle the exercise bike with his legs for 10 minutes by himself. The bike has the ability to indicate when it was doing the work or when John was doing it – and John was definitely doing it! This was such a huge step in his healing! That same day he stood in the standing frame for 20 minutes! Then, the therapist put a balloon in front of him and asked him to swat it away, and he did.

This second phase at TIRR was moving along quickly as John began to show more and more improvement in mobility and cognitive responsive-ness. He was beginning to do so much more with the right side of his body. April helped John use his right hand to shave, clean his face and pick up objects. The left side of his body wasn't coming back as quickly, but with a right-sided brain injury, we were told that is very common. However, we knew the left side would come along as well in time.

We never heard anything negative from the therapists at TIRR. They never said things like, "Oh, that's what happens with that type of injury, he just has to deal with it." Instead they said things like, "Give it some time, keep working him out and don't give up!" So, we persevered and had John do new things every day. First, we started with making him stand and bare weight on his weak and skinny legs. Next, we had the right leg moving more and trying to take steps, so we got a walker setup. This was all before his left leg would do anything.

It was so great to see the transformation of his movements from week to week. At first his right leg would barely swing forward, and the therapists had to practically move the left leg manually. We held his arms in place on the walker and even tried to hold his head up. It sometimes took three or four people to get John situated to walk. Eventually, we saw the left leg move slightly after being given an initial nudge. This was so exciting to see! John's stamina was limited, and after a few steps of walking, he was ready to sit down; so someone always had to follow behind him with his wheelchair.

We began to notice that John was becoming more aware of his surroundings. One time when they were transferring him without the electric lift, he reached out for a bar that was in front of him, as if to steady himself. That was huge and totally unexpected, but such a good sign! We continued praying over his speech that his voice and words would come forth! We were asking God to reconnect and re-wire the speech center of his brain. Mostly, though, we were praising God for the great things He had already done!

See, I have set before you today life and good, death and evil, in that I command you today to love the LORD your God, to walk in His ways, and to keep His commandments, His statutes, and His judgments, that you may live and multiply; and the LORD your God will bless you in the land which you go to possess.

Deuteronomy 30:15-16 NKJV

• • •

KEYS TO WALKING OUT A MIRACLE:

1. Testify, testify, testify what the Lord is doing.
2. Watch the Lord build new paths and connections.

Miracle Testimony

Michael Gettleman
Julie Welch

I want to share a few thoughts about my friend, John Keller. When first I met John, he did not know it. I saw him change and evolve through dark periods of his life that remain a mystery to him. It may sound strange to befriend a man when he cannot reciprocate, but that was my role as his Speech Pathologist.

John's injury caused many of his basic systems to shut down, and his survival alone was miraculous. His recovery from that point was even more inspiring. At TIRR, we watched him progress in areas of alertness, responsiveness, ambulation, communication, swallowing and functional activities. He went from someone who needed others to do literally everything for him to a man who could do for himself. We watched him progress from patient back to husband and father and son and almost everything else that he was before. Who knows what the future holds for John Keller? I know that his every step and word and act inspires me to be a better clinician, father, husband, friend and man every day.

Michael Gettleman, M.A., CCC-SLP
Speech-Language Pathologist
TIRR/Memorial Hermann

• • •

Julie Welch

I was John's physical therapist during his second admission to TIRR Memorial Hermann. He had recently had his Intrathecal Baclofen pump put in and was returning for more rehabilitation. At this time, he was completely dependent and continued to have severe spasticity in his entire body. As his medication was adjusted, John received therapy and slowly began standing and walking again. However, once John had the ability to walk with assistance, he constantly tried to sit down. Working with John was a battle of wills at times - mine vs. John's. He wanted to sit down or lie down on the floor, and it didn't matter where we were at the moment. So I had to physically prevent him from doing this. Sometimes I won and other times he did. The first time he came back to visit us, he said to me, "You were the one that wouldn't let me sit down."

There are several moments of John's journey that I will never forget. However, the most touching moment was the day John went home. His wife, April, called me on their way home. They had stopped at a restaurant, and John walked in with his family. His son, Caden, was starting to walk away, and John told him to stay close. This was coming from the same person that laid down on the floor in the middle of the gym about a week before, because he was tired. On this day, John not only walked out of the hospital, but he began his journey back to being a father.

John's recovery has truly been a miracle. He has an incredible family whose faith is a witness to all who are in their presence. They were with John throughout his entire journey and always had a smile to share with anyone who was around. They will always have a special place in my heart.

Chapter 18

Reconnecting for the Finish

James Keller

W ay back at the beginning of this journey, we were given the promise that John would live and not die and stand to declare the things of God. We all prayed for that promise to be revealed quickly, maybe even instantly. However, we soon learned that God's timetable is not always as we expect. We had to seek God more diligently and stand on the promise we were given, because now we were getting closer to the place of fulfillment. God was truly doing what He said He would do! John was showing us daily how much he could do. The reconnections the Lord brought forth in John during this time were just awesome.

It was so evident to us that John wanted to move forward faster than his abilities would allow at the time, so we asked everyone to pray with us for John to have patience and keep a positive attitude with all his therapy and repetitive tasks. We could see that by God's grace he was leaping forward in his healing each day.

Maria and Erasmo Mendez, who both work with John in our corporate office, visited John one weekend. They decided to test John's new skills using some of the color and shape cards in his room. Maria asked him to find the square, triangle, circle, etc., and he did it every time. She decided to ask something more challenging. She put the colored cards in front of him and asked him to point to the color of his truck. He pointed correctly to the white card. Then she asked him the color of his Mercedes, and he pointed correctly to the black card. Next, she asked April's favorite color, and he pointed to purple! They were thrilled and told him how proud they were of him.

John was so much stronger the physical therapists stood him up without using the standing frame. He took some practice steps – not actually walking steps - but he moved his right leg forward and put it back down. Then with a little assistance, he moved his left leg up, forward and back down. He continued to do this for several repetitions. Because he did so well, his therapist said she was going to work on getting him into the standing harness and start working with him to walk in it. The next step would be to move to the treadmill.

WOW! We stand in awe of HOW GREAT OUR GOD IS! We declare over John that his head will be lifted and words of life will begin to flow out of his mouth.

> *But you are a shield around me, O LORD; you bestow glory on me and lift up my head.*
>
> Psalm 3:3 NIV

"Whose report will we believe? We will believe the report of the Lord!" This has been the battle cry of this journey to John's recovery. Each and every time something new happened, it had a domino effect. Rejoicing started with the family, and all the wonderful people at TIRR, and trickled down through the blog and then to the believers who were praying and watching with us. The believers then took it and passed it through their own churches and websites.

People following the blog were becoming "addicted" as one person put it. Some were checking the blog more than once daily for any kind of an update. By this time in the journey, there had been over 100,000 hits on the blog from countries all over the world. The encouragement being communicated because of John's progress was incredible, and it was contagious!

Then came the words everyone had been longing to hear: John walked lots and lots of steps with a walker! And, if that wasn't big enough news by itself, he is sipping out of a straw. He doesn't always swallow but knowing he wants something to drink and how to drink from a straw is a big accomplishment.

John continued to show April and everyone around just how much he was working and trying to do all that was asked of him. April found that John liked to do tasks that have meaning/significance to him; like shaving, cleaning his face, using a Q-tip to clean his ears and other such tasks. He performed all of these tasks correctly when she asked.

Even with the Baclofen pump in place, John was still having tension in his neck. He was scheduled to receive another injection of Botox in his neck to release the tension and allow more mobility in his head, neck, throat, tongue, jaw, and mouth.

We decided to use another doctor and got his appointment moved up. During the procedure, the doctor asked how he tolerated the last treatment. When Jan told him John did just great, the doctor gave John as much as she could all in his neck and upper torso. The very next day he moved his head while he was shaving. After that, he continued to have more movement and flexibility in his neck and shoulders, along with the entire left side of his body, which was doing better and with more movement occurring every day.

John amazed us on all fronts. He proudly showed us how well he was starting to move his left leg. He was still experiencing some drowsiness so the TIIR team continued to adjust his meds and decrease the flow from his pump. A new twist was that John appeared to be trying to get out of bed by himself. In physical therapy he showed them how he could get up on all fours when lying on his stomach. He, also, demonstrated how much control and movement he was capable of with his whole body. This was not something they had seen from him before. The therapists were very impressed.

A day full of laughs and new accomplishments started one morning during speech therapy. The therapist gave him a pen and showed him how to use it to click once for "yes" and twice for "no." He liked it because it was easier to use than the other clicker he had. He clicked it with his thumb, finger, other hand, off of his chin, etc. It was great to see. Next they asked him to type his name on the keyboard. He wrote JOHN, which was good. This was a start with expectations of more progress to follow.

During lunch April always gave him the chance to sip water from a straw, which he was pretty good at by now. Then she asked him if he would like some of her cracker. He grabbed it, put it in his mouth and crunched it up. Although he didn't really swallow too much of it, he obviously liked eating it, because he just kept chewing and chewing.

In occupational therapy, April told the therapist all John had done earlier. John still had the pen in his hand, so his therapist said, "John, why don't you ever write my name?" April said, "OK, John, write, "HI KATIE," and he did it! When she moved on to stretching out his neck, John did not like it at all. So, she told John if he wanted her to stop, then he needed to write STOP on the paper, and she would. He did it!

A very dear, long-time friend of John's came to visit and spend some time with him. Jan said that for the first time since the accident, she saw John really smile – a great big smile – not a halfway one. His face was loosening up and he was expressing emotion again.

Toward the end of November, John was taken into a private evaluation session with the TIRR team. Jan was asked to wait outside. We don't know all that they did, but they liked what they saw and extended John's discharge date to January 18th.

One of the questions we later found out they asked John was, "Is your schedule too packed?" He responded "No" with his clicker. Some new therapy classes were added. In one of them, he got to play Uno with other patients. He loved the competitive setting and did really good. He played better and faster each time thereafter.

December was full of marvelous accomplishments for John. He started using his left leg more and was able to get up on all fours on the exercise mat. He would come up from a sitting position and stand up using his body strength and a shopping cart for balance. He was at the point where he could transfer into his chair from the bed. He became so mobile, the night nurse found him sitting up on the side of his bed with his feet on the floor. We had always prayed for the night nurse to hear the voice of the Lord, and she actually walked in on John and kept him from falling and hurting himself. God is so faithful! He didn't have the physical strength yet to get up on his own without some supervision. So, for his protection they put a tent over his bed at night. He really did *not* like that tent.

> *It shall come to pass that before they call, I will answer; and while they are still speaking, I will hear.*
>
> Isaiah 65:24 NKJV

As John got the hang of walking, we began to see his left leg and arm move more meaningfully, and his walking became more natural looking. John began doing more on his own and needed less help. He even graduated from big walkers, to smaller walkers, to just walking with the therapists.

• • •

April Keller

When we began walking with John without any walkers, we pushed him hard. He tried to sit often, but with the therapist behind him and me in front, we would not let him. We held him up or I put my knees against his legs and tried to hold him up. All the while we were encouraging him to keep going, he was giving us his hand sign to sit. He ended up sitting on one of the therapists' laps most times, because we didn't get the chair there in time. We kept pushing him to do more to build up his strength and stamina.

Every day John walked more and more. Between his therapists and me, each day was more impressive. John's improvement was happening so rapidly that plans were changing and orders for equipment were cancelled because it was not needed anymore. God was now starting to roll with John! The amazing thing was that that all of this walking started while both of John's legs were cast up to his knee from his tendon lengthening surgery. After six weeks, the casts were removed, but he continued to wear boots to hold the foot position in place. These plastic boots rubbed a huge blister on his left foot, but John continued to improve and nothing was stopping him from progressing.

Another huge step in John's advancement was his ability to communicate with everyone. One Saturday afternoon, I asked him several questions but could not read what he was writing. I asked again and he wrote it again, but I still couldn't read it. He underlined his words for emphasis but to no avail. Needless to say, we both were frustrated. So, I merely asked John, "Can you nod your head for 'yes' or shake it for 'no?'" And then, as I looked into his eyes, praying under my breath for any kind of movement, John nodded! Oh my gosh! I was so excited! I began asking him more questions!

I remembered his occupational therapist was working, so I wheeled him down and around the gym to find her. I told the therapist what John was doing, and she asked him a question. He nodded "yes" for her too! We were so excited! This was an even better means of communication! All I could think about was: *Wait till I show his speech therapist - he will love this!*

John had come so far in communicating with us. He started with blinking his eyes, which didn't always reveal a true pattern. Once his hands were moving we tried one finger for "yes" or two for "no," clicking a pen, clicking a mouse, touching a screen that said "yes, no, or I don't know", then to writing, and finally nodding. John had come a LONG way but this was just the beginning!

• • •

Blog December 18, 2008:

Boy, has it been a week full of miracles, signs, and wonders for John. He is now being called "The Miracle," and everyone at TIRR is proclaiming that what they are seeing in him is only because of God's greatness. They are overwhelmingly amazed. He turns on and can use his electric razor, toothbrush, and massage wand by himself. He can, also, use his legs and right arm/hand to wheel himself around in his chair. He is standing and reaching more during therapy. At a memory class called recreation therapy, they asked him questions like: Where was Jesus born? He wrote Jerusalem. In what? A manger. What color is Santa's beard? White. Where does Santa live? North Pole. How great is that?

John went on a field trip to Target. He headed over to the CD aisle and pointed out a CD that he liked. Next, they headed to the toys for Dalton's and Caden's gifts. When they went to check out, he put the items on the conveyor belt, swiped the credit card through the machine, and picked up his package by himself. Then he rode home sitting on the bus seat, not in his wheelchair.

He is getting a day pass for December 27th, and we will celebrate Christmas together at the apartment in Houston. That will be so nice! They are working on stimulating his speech, and he is going to start some new therapy sessions focusing on this area. We are sure there is still some healing and loosening of the muscles and vocal cords that need to happen, so he can eat and speak.

• • •

James Keller

In order for John to go to the apartment in Houston for a Christmas celebration with the family, we had to learn how to get John in and out of the wheelchair and in and out of a car. Everyone gathered for the lessons in the parking lot. John did just great. He held onto the top of the passenger door that was open. Then he sat down and brought his feet inside and reached up to buckle his own seat belt. When we knew we had that down pretty good, we were ready to go back inside, but John was ready to go in the car. Jan said, "We are sorry John, but we were just practicing how to get you in and out of the car." He was very upset with us.

The family planned to celebrate Christmas with John on December 27th and we were all excited. As we left TIRR, we noticed how much John enjoyed riding in the car and looking at all his new surroundings. We wondered what was on his mind. We couldn't wait for him to see the apartment and all the family gathered together.

We brought in some food from our favorite Mexican restaurant in Houston, Lupe Tortillas. When we all ate, John even had a taste, but at this time, he wasn't able to eat much regular food. We still had to feed him through his pegtube.

We got him out of his wheelchair and on to the couch. He wanted to switch seats often...trying to get comfortable. We helped him to stand a bit when he was restless. He really just watched everyone and the kids interact and did great with so much noise and activity in the small, two-bedroom apartment. We kept asking him if he wanted to rest, but he stayed in the living room with all of us. Everyone watched as we helped him opened his gifts. He kept trying to smell his cologne – only to find out later he couldn't smell anything yet. John says he doesn't remember that day with us, but we all will remember it forever. We rejoiced at being able to celebrate Christmas with him.

When it was time to return to TIRR, we never considered that John would think he was going to stay at the apartment so we weren't expecting him to be upset. When we pulled up in front of TIRR, I went to help him out of the car, and John shook his head "No!" We explained that he had to stay one more month at TIRR because he wanted to be able to walk out on his own, and he was not walking well enough just yet to do that.

At this time, John would stand up beside his chair for a minute or two and then sit back down. He sometimes stood up with the wheelchair attached to him. This is when everyone started calling him "Turtle Man," because he could be seen walking down the hallway with the wheelchair strapped to his backside like a turtle shell.

• • •

Blog January 1, 2009:

HAPPY NEW YEAR! The family gathered in Houston to spend Christmas with John. What an amazing sight to see! He is moving, standing, walking, hugging, nodding his head yes and no, doing what is asked of him and getting better every day. We all just cried when we saw him standing. He lifted three laundry detergent bottles filled with various amounts of water up over his head. And they didn't hand them to him. He had to squat down, pick them up, and then lift them over his head.

He has started crossing his legs and is working so hard to get better so he can walk out of TIRR come the end of January. He wants to work constantly to better himself. It really does blow you away to see him continually trying. They have approved him to work on standing in his room when he is not in therapy sessions. He wants to do it all the time. So they have worked out a plan that he is allowed to stand and then has to sit for three minutes before trying again. Otherwise, he will just keep sitting and standing continually - even with his seat belt buckled in his wheelchair! It's almost funny, except for the fact that it just goes to show you how strong he really is. That chair weighs about 80 pounds, and he lifts it with no problem.

During workouts he gets his weight machine situated and ready to go. Then they tell him to do ten reps and off he goes. They don't even count out loud for him, but when he gets to ten he stops. This shows that he is counting them off in his head.

We got to hear a testimony from of one of his doctors confessing that according to John's CT scan he is truly amazed at what John is doing. He said he didn't expect to see him so awake, alert, and playing on the computer trying to get on the internet. And another doctor said he believes John will be talking before the one year anniversary of the accident. We stand in agreement with these doctors and proclaim, "Lord, let these things come. In Jesus' name!"

• • •

KEYS TO WALKING OUT A MIRACLE:

1. Seek God more diligently and stand on the promise you were given, when you are getting closer to the place of fulfillment.

2. Pray to have patience and keep a positive attitude as you wait on the Lord to complete His work.

Testimony 18

Miracle Testimony

Judy Toscano

A nurse's dilemma is always to be at the right place at the right time. It's a quandary that motivates me to pray for each patient on my unit as I drive the 45 minutes on the Houston freeways to work. Fortunately at night, I am surrounded by other prayer warriors who do the same. That is a big part of why I have stayed at TIRR the past 12 years. Many on the nursing staff inspire me to more compassionate care as I watch them attend to the needs of patients as if they were their own children or parent. On this unit as individuals emerge from comas, it is fairly common for the staff to struggle with being hit, bitten, spat on and sworn at. Not every patient emerges this way, but it is a frequent occurrence. I marvel at how well the staff handles it and continue to love and graciously care for those who come to us from all over the world. We watch as God works miracles in small and large ways.

John Keller came to PCU3 at TIRR as one of our worst case scenarios. I cared for him from day one, and I don't recall him being able to do anything, not even track with his eyes. However, John didn't go through the usual combative stage we have learned to expect when a patient comes out of a coma. John emerged from a minimally responsive stage very peacefully, like awakening from a winter of hibernation. He simply woke up slowly moving through recovery with each *day bringing another small miracle. I remember thinking: What a shame; he is young, handsome, has a lovely wife and two small children. It brought tears to my eyes. I was struggling with the current reality but was, also, reminded that faith doesn't operate by what we see but by believing the promises of God. So, I began to pray for John quoting verses I was memorizing: Ephesians 3:20, "... now to Him who is able to do exceedingly abundantly more than we ask according to the power that is in us..." and Psalm 138:8, "The Lord will perfect that which concerns me." I'll never forget how John and his family touched my life and taught me so much more about faith. Their positive attitude toward John and their constant praise of the staff motivated all of us to even greater faith for his situation.*

At night, I was continually reminded as I looked at John and all the family pictures on the walls that he was a son, a husband and a father to someone. It made me want to watch over him as if he was my own son and make sure nothing went wrong on my shift. This meant vigilantly checking on him through the night, as well as knowing his labs, medications and his progress notes for the week. One night as I was charting, I felt an urge to check on John. As I walked to his room, I remembered the many nights I had to put bi-valves and splints on John's extremities to prevent contractures. Sometimes it took 20 minutes to put them on and to cover over areas to prevent breakdown from excessive rubbing. It would have been easier to ignore this protocol, but knowing that I wanted what was best for John, compelled me to keep utilizing the splints. When I stepped into his room that night, he was one step from getting out of bed. He would certainly have fallen, potentially causing a fracture, a new brain hemorrhage or a concussion. All I could say was, "Thank you, God, for bringing me here." Several times during his stay an internal prompting found John needing something; suctioning, pain meds, a brief change or turning. Jan frequently called at night to see how he was doing, and I was always glad to walk down to make sure all was well.

John's family taught me how important encouragement is to everyone. They were so positive and sure of John's recovery that it became infectious. This experience affirmed my belief that faith and hope are keys to the healing process. They were, also, very effusive in their praise of the nursing staff, which made us all the more determined to press for John's recovery.

Judy Toscano, R.N.
TIRR, PCU3

Miracle 18

Final Rewards

Jan Keller

As the New Year of 2009 dawned, John just kept moving forward, moving forward, moving forward. He was working constantly on standing and walking. In fact, that seemed to be all he was focused on. He was restless and having a hard time focusing and sitting still. He had grown tired of TIRR and was ready to get home to a more familiar setting. It was decided John would leave TIRR on January 29th to go home. John was really working hard toward that goal and continued to amaze everyone with whom he came in contact.

> *For every child of God defeats this evil world and we achieve*
> *this victory through our faith.*
>
> I John 5:4 NLT

When James arrived in Houston for a visit, John thought he would be going home since his dad was there. He went from door-to-door in his wheelchair. We asked if he wanted to go outside, and he nodded yes. Once outside, we let him throw the basketball. He stood and threw it twelve times before he tired and sat down. We had to explain once more that it wasn't quite time yet to go home.

TIRR was really accommodating with John toward the end of his stay. All indications showed that John was growing weary of therapy. If he didn't want to go for therapy, the therapist said, "That's okay, but if you will do this one thing for me, then I will not ask anything more." John would nod and do what he was asked to do.

By this time, John had an air mattress on the floor to sleep on. This was safer because he kept trying to climb out of the tent on his bed that was meant to protect him from falling. He hated being restricted. With the mattress on the floor, he could get up, pull himself to the chair and back to the mattress on his own. He kept his shoes on all the time, because it gave him traction to do what he wanted to do.

John was strong and determined to do everything by himself, but he still was not walking without a trained therapist or technician. I told him, "John, I cannot walk with you because I am not licensed yet." He remembers me telling him that before he was talking again and said it didn't make sense to him at all.

John went through an aggressive stage at this time and was often irritated. The doctor's report said that John had lost the filter in the brain that tells him how to treat people. We had not seen this behavior previously, and we declared that he did have a filter, the Holy Spirit, and everything would be filtered through Him. We were told that John might cuss and say profane things and that he might pull out his feeding tube, or possibly fall and hurt himself. We said, "Not on our watch will these things happen." We continued to pray that all things were working for John's good.

The nurses were concerned that in his frustration, John would try to pull his pegtube (feeding tube) out of his stomach or injure himself in some other way, so they decided to put mittens on him. I made the comment that the mittens would not be on John's hands for long, to which the response was, "Oh no, he will not get those off." Within minutes, John was tucking them under his arms and pulling them off. A compromise was offered. They simply asked John not to pull at the pegtube and agreed they would not make him wear the mittens if he complied. John agreed. The pegtube was left alone, and the mittens went away.

John tells us now that he remembers being restrained and hated it. He could not understand why he was in lock-down. He would go to the locked double doors and kick at them. It helped that someone from the family was always there with him, because the nurses were worried he would get hurt from being on the move so much.

On January 21, 2009 John was introduced to a new occupational therapist. She asked John, pointing toward me, "Who is that?" John looked at me, looked back at the therapist and, without hesitation, said, "Mom." I looked at John and through tears said, "Look John, there it is, you found your voice." Then I said, "If you can say that, you can say, 'Praise the Lord.'" The next words John spoke were "Praise the Lord" and then "Hallelujah!"

I said, "Let's call April!"

• • •

April Keller

Jan called me and told me to call John, and said he wanted to speak to me. I had talked to John before on the phone, but usually I would talk, and he would just listen. As I dialed the phone and heard him say, "Hello," I could not believe my ears! John was talking! By the time I got back to Houston, he was talking in full sentences.

• • •

Jan Keller

John and I were sitting on John's bed when John and April hung up from their phone call. He looked at me and said, "Can I use your cell phone?" I said, "Of course you can, but why?" John said, "I have to call Dad and tell him I am talking!"

Anyone who knows James will tell you that he is a man with a heart for the things of God, but how much more so when it was his own son. This walk had truly been a test of faith for him - like no other he had ever experienced. He learned early on that he had to let go of everything and completely and unconditionally trust God.

• • •

James Keller

I had just come back to the Valley from Houston for a few days. My son-in-law and I were driving down the expressway in the early afternoon, and my phone rang. I recognized Jan's number and didn't think anything about it really. I answered the phone and was shocked to hear John say, "Hey, Dad!" I choked up and as tears began to roll down my cheeks. I replied, "John! It's good to hear your voice!" The next words were the best words I could have ever heard when John said, "I love you, Dad!" Of course, by now, I'm crying all over the place and trying to drive at the same time, so I told John I was going to have to pull over before I had an accident. I could not see the road because of the tears of joy that were streaming down my face!"

• • •

Jan Keller

John continued to call friends and family that day to tell them about this miracle! While he was on the phone with one person, the other line would ring, and he would hand the phone back to me and point to it so I could switch over to the other line!

Eventually it was time for me to go and get something to eat. In my absence, John asked to use his nurse's cell phone. The nurse looked at him and said, "What if I don't have a cell phone?" John replied, "Everyone has a cell phone." With that, the nurse let John use the phone.

John called me. The amazing thing about this particular phone call was that John remembered my cell phone number. He heard me recite the number to the nurse when I left, and he remembered it. He called to see where I was and when I was coming back. And it wasn't just my number he remembered – John remembered everyone's phone number.

Just as in the beginning, word spread fast through the community of family and friends. By now, prayer warriors worldwide had joined in prayer over the course of the previous eleven months. Here is the joyful message that went around the world:

• • •

Blog January 21, 2009:
John spoke today! After talking to Jan, April and James, John went on to tell them that today was "Wednesday" and tomorrow is "Thursday." Of course, he still has a long way to go. But his voice is back, and this is a big hurdle in his healing.

If you remember the surgeon in the Valley confessed that he believed John would talk before the one-year anniversary of the accident. Praise the Lord, we all prayed and believed and asked God to bring it to pass! And He did! Hallelujah!

• • •

One of the first things John did after he started talking was to ask a nurse for her badge. When he was given the badge to see what he would do with it, John went straight to the elevator in his wheelchair, scanned the badge, got on the elevator and announced he was ready to go home! Everyone was surprised how he put that together in his mental processing – using the elevator required an employee badge.

The doctor came to see John after she learned he was talking. She asked him numerous questions, and John answered her correctly. When she asked him about the names of the therapists and nurses, he did get some of the therapists' names confused. Then she asked him the name of the president, and John responded, "Barack Obama!" Everyone was really surprised since the election had occurred after John's accident, and the inauguration had just taken place.

At that time, April was coming to Houston for the weekend, and John was really excited to see her now that he was talking. She texted me a message saying she was getting close. He wanted to stand up and greet her with a big hug when she came into his room. I left the room and let them share some quality time.

• • •

April Keller

It was a Saturday and John's brother, Charles, was in town just a few days after John started talking. John and Charles were always picking on each other about something. I had just gotten to Houston and was so excited to see and hear John talk. He was cracking jokes and being rather funny. Charles was thirsty and wanted to get a drink from the vending machine. So, off we went downstairs. Charles got his Dr. Pepper, and I can't remember if John said anything about wanting some, or if I just said, "John, why don't you try it?" As we mentioned before, he had been drinking a little from a straw, and he was able to eat some chunky soup, but that was it. As I lowered the Dr. Pepper closer to him, he put it to his lips, tipped his head back and took a big gulp...with NO spills! This was huge!

When we went back to his room, I asked the weekend nurse if we could get a tray that night of slightly chopped food. She was hesitant but finally agreed. I had already been approved by our speech therapist to feed John. So this is how it started...he ate a ton! I showed the nurse and asked if we could get an order for more normal food that was slightly chopped not pureed. John did great with it and was able to feed himself, too, if I made him. I said, "You can move your hands and arms, let's do this...!" He said, "Well if you're willing to feed me then, I'll let you." I said, "No, I've got 2 kids at home to feed, you're a grown man...feed yourself." I pushed him, but I think he needed it. We were so thankful this happened before he was scheduled to be discharged from TIRR. No more...tube feedings! We were done with that!

• • •

Jan Keller

The TIRR staff was just as excited as everyone else when John began to talk. They never gave up hope and always encouraged John to keep moving on. Someone asked me why I thought the timing of this occurred now, and I said, "We had been praying that you would see the miracle of John talking because we knew God could do it and we wanted you to rejoice with us."

TIRR brought 18 medical students in to meet John, and he shared with them about his miracle. One of them was married to an NICU nurse at The Methodist Hospital and had heard about John from his stay there.

John's college roommate, who is the basketball coach for 2nd Baptist School in Houston, came to visit. The team had been praying for John since his accident. He asked John to come to a game that week and be the "Honorary Coach." John attended in a wheelchair and sat for 2½ hours for the game. The jerseys the kids were wearing were blue with the words "Rise With Us" over a silhouette of John shooting a basketball into a hoop. After the game, John visited with the players and had a really great time.

The next day, John had more visitors, again some college roommates and friends. They were having a great time reminiscing about old times. They purposely messed up the stories as they talked, changing a little detail here or there, to see if John would catch them. Not only did John catch them, he set them straight.

The night before John was being discharged to go home, John's college roommates that lived in Houston threw him a going-away party. Of course, we had packed the video camera to take it to the party. In packing up the truck, the camera bag had been set on the bumper instead of inside the truck. As we left the apartment complex, the camera bag fell off the bumper into the street, and with it, the camera containing all of the documentation taken of John's miracle journey.

As we pulled up at a stop light, a car drove up beside us and told us about the bag falling off the bumper. When we went back to get it, it was gone. I was extremely upset, but I knew the Lord wanted the "Victory" shared. So, we declared that the Lord was in charge and whatever happened, happened for a reason; and we would still see the glory of the Lord. We asked the Lord to have the person that picked it up, call us.

At the party, we prayed again. Shortly thereafter, my cell phone rang. It was the daughter of the couple that had picked up the bag. Her parents had driven into Houston for a doctor's visit and were heading home when they spotted the black bag in the street and picked it up before it was destroyed in traffic. We were so blessed, but the miracle continued as our conversation revealed she had been a patient at TIRR and was a miracle herself. We shared and cried together!

The daughter said her parents felt badly for driving all the way home, but I assured her it would be a blessing to meet them and pick up the camera. It was then she shared that both parents were fighting cancer. I told her this was a divine appointment and made arrangements to go pray with them! Again, we had seen that the Lord was in control of every situation. He wanted us to minister to that couple, because God knew right where they were and loved them! We rejoiced that John's miracle would be shown to so many to proclaim that God is able to do that which we can never expect or think possible.

Excitement was in the air the next day, but at the same time, everyone was sad to see John go. Many friendships had been formed, and it was hard to say goodbye. God had done a mighty work in John for all to see and what an encouragement it was to those who worked in this place and witnessed patients' challenges on a daily basis. But at the end of the day, John Keller was ready to go home!

• • •

KEYS TO WALKING OUT A MIRACLE:

1. Continue to pray that all things work for good until you see the fulfillment of the miracle.

2. Continue to let go of everything and completely and unconditionally trust God to bring you through to the end.

3. Rejoice and give God the glory as you begin to reap the rewards of your prayers and perseverance.

Miracle Testimony

Charles Oney

I am John's older brother and he and I have always been best buds growing up together. We've always competed in everything we did and constantly kid each other. We would talk early in the morning almost every day about business and kids and family. John loves being busy and so do I.

When I got the call about John's accident, I flew down from Dallas to McAllen as soon as I could. Seeing my brother in a coma with a brain bleed and broken pelvis, was so awful that I cannot describe my feelings. I can't say I was full of faith, but I did agree with the family that God was going to heal John completely. I did not know or understand how or when, but I agreed with April, Mom and Dad, my two sisters and brothers-in-law, and others that God was going to do this. Through this I learned that faith means you never give up. And that is what I call "family faith" because that faith collectively is stronger than just one person's faith. I think the Bible calls it mustard seed faith. The other thing I learned is that as a parent, you will always be there for your child and that is powerful. No matter how old they get, you will always be the mom or dad. I saw that in action, and as a father of 3 children, I learned a lot as I watched our families go into action for John. I thank God for what He has done, and I thank God for families. John, brother, I love you and am glad you are back.

Chapter 20

Homeward Bound

Jan Keller

Two weeks before John's discharge date James looked at John and said, "Do you want to *walk* out of here?" John shook his head, "Yes." Every Friday, during this entire journey, all 350 of the employees of the family business, plus family and friends wore matching t-shirts as a way of standing in prayer for John. A word had come forth early on in this walk about Jesus being the author and finisher of John's faith and that John had not finished his race yet and had more to do. The t-shirts were black with large white letters. On the front, it said, "WOFJ," which stood for "Work Out For John," and the Hebrews 12:2 reference. On the back, it said, "Finisher."

> *Looking unto Jesus the author and finisher of our faith; who for the joy that was set before him endured the cross, despising the shame, and is set down at the right hand of the throne of God.*
>
> Hebrews 12:2 KJV

The day John was discharged from TIRR, he purposefully wore his WOFJ shirt. His nurse had the honor of cutting off John's identification armband. What a faithful and awesome God we serve! John Keller left TIRR on January 29th walking and talking and praising God!

The Rio Grande Valley is in the most southern part of Texas and sits right on the border between Texas and Mexico. From Houston to McAllen, normally a six-hour drive without stops, took nine hours to complete that day. On the way, John's entourage of two cars stopped at a restaurant, and he had his first hamburger in almost a year. Enjoying the entire hamburger and nearly devouring it in one bite, John said, "I feel normal again!"

When we were about half-way home, John called some friends that live in Corpus Christi and asked them to meet us at a stopping point about 30 miles west of Corpus. He, also, asked them to bring him a plate of double dozy (pronounced "doo-zie") cookies, and he really enjoyed them as well! All in all, John did very well with the trip home until the last hour when he was anxiously ready to be out of the vehicle.

All through this walk, April and I said we would know exactly what the Lord wanted us to do because He would show us. In praying about taking John home, James and I knew that it would be very difficult for April with her three-year-old and one-year-old boys to take care of John alone. He still needed constant supervision and considerable personal care, and James and I knew we could best handle that at our house until he was better prepared to go home with his family.

John was so happy to be home, and everyone was grateful to have him back. He was talking more and more and remembered everyone. The first day at home, he spent a lot of time walking and enjoyed watching his kids play outside. He even went for a few rides in the golf cart while holding Dalton, his youngest son.

We recognized immediately that John had to get re-oriented with the layout of the house. He kept saying he could not see, but we knew that it was not because of his vision. The issue was that his brain was not firing fast enough for his eyes to catch up with the movement of his body.

We saw so many beautiful things the Lord was doing for us. John did not need a hospital bed since our guest room had space for a mattress on the floor, and he was already comfortable with that. During the day, he began to rest on our king-sized bed, and he liked it. He never had a problem getting in and out of it, and before long, he was back to sleeping in a regular bed.

John was eating normal food and had not used the pegtube since he had been home. He was able to swallow all his medications in pill-form as well. Before the accident, John ate small meals, four-to-six times a day. Now, he was eating three bowls of cereal and three waffles for breakfast. He said, "Don't worry Mom, I will slow it down in a few weeks. It's just that everything tastes so good!"

Another blessing was that from the day John came home, he didn't need the wheelchair. He was walking and getting around with someone by his side to assist him. It was incredible to see how far he had come and what a miracle he was, but his stamina was not there yet. As long as he rested when he felt he needed to, moving around inside the house was never an issue. We set chairs along the hallway from the bedrooms to the main part of the house so he could sit down when necessary. The unused wheelchair was shipped back to Houston on the one-year anniversary of his accident.

When it came time to locate a therapy tech to work with John at home, God had someone already in place. Rick, a tech who had worked with John at TIRR, had moved to our area a few months before John's discharge. He called to see how John was doing. As we talked, Rick said he liked his job, but it was mostly with children, and his heart was really in working with adults. So, I asked if he would pray about working with John on a daily basis, and he said he would. Rick came to visit on the Sunday after John came home, and he started to work with John the next day. Rick was an answer to prayer, because he told John that the Lord put them together first as Christian brothers. He has been an inspiration to all of us. We thank the Lord for dedicated people called with servant's hearts.

After John settled in at home, people from his business connections began coming by to see him. They were so surprised that John remembered all of their names and even what kind of car they drove. He had visitors from his high school days, as well as college friends.

One day, John's brother Charles was flying in from Dallas. On the way to the airport to pick him up, John started giggling. I asked what that was all about, and he said, "Charles is going to have a limp!" Charles had been playing basketball and actually had torn his Achilles' tendon but had not seen a doctor yet. John said, "I am going to call him gimp!" So, the weekend began with teasing that only brothers can do.

John woke up every day with a zeal for life, saying, "This is what's happening today…" and went about doing it. He was ready to do whatever was planned for him. We had to be creative because we did not want to call it "therapy." We simply wanted to help increase his attention span and stay focused on what needed to be done. Rick established some "landmarks" throughout the house for John, such as a flower arrangement outside the door meant turn left to the bedroom. It didn't take long for John to become familiar with everything at the house again.

Another obstacle John had to deal with was the urge to go to the restroom thirty times a day, but he found a way to turn it into a laughing matter. He named the process, "The Urge," giving it a personality until he tamed it and brought it under control.

April and the boys came over every day, and she helped Rick work out John while I kept the boys busy. April, John and Rick would run errands in some of the larger stores, which kept John interested in walking. At first, John tired easily. One day, he asked if there was a place to sit, to which the answer was, "No." John wasn't buying it, and said, "Don't tell me that. There are dressing rooms here, and they have benches in them where I can sit."

After a month of working out at the house, John let it be known he was ready to return to the gym. John and Rick began going to the gym twice a day, sometimes three. He has always been very passionate about working out and was now cleared to return to the gym.

Over the course of the next few weeks, many blessings became evident of how God's hand was very much in this miracle in progress. On February 8, 2009 April took John to the company office to visit everyone. Just like my dream on the morning of the accident, John climbed the flight of 23 stairs to get to the office on the 2nd floor. When he walked through the door with James, everyone was gathered to welcome him with a big round of applause.

John sat in his office and remembered his computer password. He remembered certain reports he used to create and what they meant. Later he visited all of the stores, and the managers and staff cried and were so touched when John walked in and talked with them.

Prior to the accident, John had become a very serious man with all of the stresses of life and running a business. But the humor now being witnessed is that of a young John Keller. His sense of humor never fails to bring laughter to him and those around him. When he tells people about his accident, he says, "It knocked me into a different zip code!"

It was mind blowing to see God's hand at work in John's life as he continued to improve by leaps and bounds each day. Shortly after arriving home, John and the family attended the Annual Mayor's Prayer Luncheon held by the City of McAllen. The speaker shared his testimony and said his prayer was to be a person who touched peoples' lives. He, also, mentioned that God is always working for our good. Barney Sarver, our close friend, was there to accept the first Community Service Award ever given out by the City in honor of his wife, Cheri, whose life was tragically taken in a car accident on June 12, 2008. She was like a mother to our kids and a precious friend to all of us. She even had the students at the school where she was the principal praying for John every day for his healing. As Barney accepted the award, he asked our family to stand. John stood and what a testimony of answered prayer that was for the City to see!

About six weeks after returning home, the area where the pump was inserted into John's abdomen was inflamed and swollen. He went to the local doctor, but they kept telling him it looked fine. We decided it was time the doctor in Houston had a look at it, so we emailed some pictures to Houston. Within a day, John was on a plane to Houston to see the doctor and was immediately admitted to The Methodist Hospital. He was put on strong antibiotics and watched carefully. This type of pump can work its way through the abdominal wall and then be susceptible to a greater chance of infection. Our trust was in the Lord, and we knew He was in control.

Again, we had to believe: All things work out for good for those that love the Lord because God's timing is always perfect. While we were at Methodist Hospital, I knew there was a strong possibility we would run into the doctor that had originally taken John as a patient, so I had eyes to see. As John and I were out walking in the hall, I caught the doctor's eye as we passed the nurses' station and his mouth dropped open. He remembered us, and I said, "John, would you like to say something to this gentleman? This is the doctor that you never met. He took you as a patient back at the beginning."

John began to thank the doctor for all of the care he had received. He said that he did not remember anything and was so thankful to the Lord because He knew John did not like pain. The doctor was amazed at John's progress and recovery. The Lord quickened my spirit and said, "See? My perfect timing…what you thought was an inconvenience to come to Houston and have the pump revisioned became a testimony of My complete healing in John. Everything works together for good. Even My grace can cover any mistakes that have been made. Trust Me and watch Me perform My healing in John."

We, also, came across the teaching Resident who helped us by explaining procedures and answering questions when John was in the Neurosurgery ICU. He remembered John immediately and said that because of John's miraculous comeback, he has completely changed the way he looks at traumatic brain injuries now. Again, we gave God all of the glory!

A Welcome Home "Miracles DO Happen" BBQ was held in McAllen, and John was greeted by over 350 family members and friends. John was in charge of blowing up all the balloons with the helium tank and spent the rest of the day talking and visiting with everyone – with a perfect memory intact. He knew who people were, how long he had known them, and remembered details about them from the past.

On another trip to Houston, John was able to go back to see all of the people at The University Place Nursing Center. When he left there, he had not been walking or talking. As he walked off the elevator, all of the staff realized who he was, and there was much rejoicing. They were so blessed to see and talk with him.

After visiting the doctor at TIRR, it was agreed John's medications would be gradually decreased, and by the end of May 2009, he was completely off all medications, except for the Baclofen pump. Only God could do this!

The Baclofen pump medication was being gradually decreased on a weekly basis with the goal in sight of complete removal. This was unheard of since it was customary that once a pump was placed, it was there for life. Later in the summer, another visit to the doctor in Houston was necessary because the pump was no longer releasing medication. The doctor realized an infection had set into the tissue around the pump, and the decision was made to remove it. John underwent his 14th and final surgery since his accident, when the Baclofen pump was removed on August 20, 2009 less than a year after it was inserted. John had declared all along it would come out in less than a year. God was in control and everything was in His hands. John was now totally medication free.

We continued to stand firm knowing God was continuing to complete His good work of healing and restoration in John. His sense of smell began to return, but his eyesight and cognitive short term memory skills were still a work in progress.

I don't watch TV during the day, but one day, God prompted me to turn it on to one of the morning shows. It just happened to be featuring a lady who was sharing about a computer program, called Brain Fit www.Lumonsity.com. It was developed by a woman who had been in a bad car accident and needed this type of therapy for herself. This was such an answer to prayer, and it was exactly the type of tool John needed. He began working with the program two hours each day on his computer, and it has improved his cognitive skills, memory and vision significantly. I have learned to follow those promptings from the Lord: Obey! Don't Delay!

Over the summer John began going home with April and the boys for a day or two at a time. This allowed him to gradually become acclimated to their house and get to know Caden and Dalton after being absent from their lives for over a year. By late fall he was more independent and had fully transitioned back home permanently in time to spend the holidays with April and the boys.

Since returning home, when asked questions that he can't answer, he is quick to comment that he wouldn't have known that answer even before the brain injury! Again, his humor is ever present and such a delight to witness.

For John each and every day is better than the last. He hears better, listens better, and has more compassion for people. He loves telling his story to everyone who will listen. Before the accident he was more reserved, but now he strikes up conversations easily, asking questions and offering opinions. He frequently says, "Don't ask me to tell you something unless you want to hear the truth." He speaks the truth of God's love and is so thankful to be alive.

In the beginning John developed a rather unique way of telling his story to people he met. He started by saying, "If you have the time, I would like to share an analogy." Most people agree to hear him out. Then he says, "There is a NASCAR driver that has a bad accident and hits the wall with his car. He is wearing a helmet, is using a HANS device (a safety feature that securely holds the driver's head and neck in place) and remains inside the car. Then, there is another other guy that is riding a motorcycle and gets hit by a car. He flies 150 feet through the air across five lanes of traffic, falls to the ground and hits his head. He does not have a helmet on. Which of these people do you think died? You cannot answer 'None of the Above' or 'All of the Above.'"

Most people respond that it is the motorcycle rider that dies. They are shocked to find out it was not the motorcycle rider who died, and John was the motorcycle rider that he was speaking of in the analogy. This opens the door for him to share the testimony of his miraculous healing.

We have been blessed to touch so many lives through the miracle of John's road to recovery. One thing we learned about walking through a miracle, it's a progressive thing. It may or may not be immediate. You have to P.U.S.H.- **P**ray **U**ntil **S**omething **H**appens! It's not about your condition; it's about your position! When you come to that place where you say, "I have done everything I can do;" God says, "Now *I* can do something!" Bad things happen to good people, but God's people can take what the enemy means for bad and turn it to good. Miracles begin with relationship. The altar is a place of exchange – the old for new and the bad for good. The fight is a fight over your faith. We have to get the enemy out of our heads and fight him with the Word – the Sword of the Spirit. Giving up is not an option when you're fighting for a miracle.

• • •

KEYS TO WALKING OUT A MIRACLE:

1. Watch as many blessings become evident of how God's hand is at work in the miracle in progress.
2. Stand firm and **P**ray **U**ntil **S**omething **H**appens, knowing God will complete His good work of healing and restoration.
3. Get it clearly established in your spirit that giving up is not an option when you're fighting for a miracle.

Miracle Testimony

Rick and Susan Myerscough

T*he healing and recovery of John is a demonstration and witness of God's faithfulness, goodness and blessing. It is, also, a testimony of the faithfulness of the Keller family to believe God and hold to His promise in the midst of fear, doubt, uncertainty, bad reports and unbelief. John's continued miracle and recovery is, also, a testimony of the power of unified prayer support and a demonstration of the love of God and the love we have for one another.*

After I learned of John's accident, I sensed in my spirit the boldness of God's promise to trust and believe for his complete recovery. John and the Keller family had many opportunities to lose hope or give in to doubt, unbelief and bad reports from well-meaning doctors, hospital staff, family members or friends, who may have shared their hope for John…but did not have the promises of God and His Word in their hearts. Without the knowledge of God's Word and will concerning John and his injuries…they could not have faith to believe God to bring John through.

"Faith comes by hearing, and hearing by the Word of God," as we read in Romans 10:17 NKJV. If you do not know what God's Word says, you cannot have

faith to believe. You have to hear it, believe it, receive it into your heart, and then act on it to see the results that God intends.

The Keller's had heard the plan of God concerning John. "John, will not die, but live." This was a Word from the Holy Spirit instilled in their spirits and backed up by the written Word of God in Psalm 118:17. The Keller family and many other family members and friends, took a stand on God's Word and did not compromise. They stood guard over John while he lay in a coma state, filtering what was allowed to be spoken over him and around him. You may think this sounds silly or strange… however, Jesus gave us an example of this very thing. He was asked to go to the house of an official of the synagogue, whose 12-year-old daughter was dying. On his way, someone reported that the girl had already died, but Jesus answered "fear." He spoke God's will concerning this young girl and stopped fear from doing its work in the ruler's heart.

When Jesus came to the house, He allowed no one to enter with him except those who believed. When He saw all were "weeping and mourning" in the house, He put them outside. Jesus had to deal with unbelief too. He protected the father, his disciples, and the plan of God by speaking and acting on God's will.

I am so glad that the Keller's and others spoke God's will concerning John and his future and the future of his family. They did not allow fear or unbelief to rule in John's situation, and I am convinced it is because of this that John is with us today…the miracle we see before us.

As John's uncle and aunt, we rejoice with John and his family and give thanks to our heavenly Father for His plan for John and April and their precious family.

Chapter 21

A Miracle of
Biblical Proportions

John Keller

This is my story and I slept through most of it. It seems strange that this could happen to anyone, but it happened to me. I love to tell people, "I got hit so hard I was knocked into a new zip code!" I went for a bike ride one day and woke up in Houston, Texas eleven months later. Unless anyone can think of another one, I tell people I am the biggest miracle of the 21st century. In fact, I am a miracle of biblical proportions. I say that not out of arrogance but out of confidence.

The day that I woke up, I sounded so strange to myself. I am beginning to remember more things now. The day I went for the ride was the most beautiful day you could ever imagine. I was in a coma for 70+ days, in three different hospitals for 11 months, and I had a total of 14 surgeries. I didn't walk, talk or eat for almost a year. I am happy to be alive. Why did God save me? I am not anymore special than any of you.

My wife is a very strong woman and was by my side the entire time. She didn't have to be. She is still by my side through the recovery process. I love her with all my heart. I feel very fortunate to have married her nine years ago – 8 years for me, because I was plumb knocked out for a whole year!

One of the things I remembered when I woke up was P.U.S.H. – Pray Until Something Happens. This was not anything I knew of from before the accident, but I found out later that this was being said around me in my room while I was asleep. Another thing that happened before I woke up was that CDs of scriptures and songs were being played in my room.

I had never heard of one of the Christian music artists before the accident, but once I was awake, I knew all of his songs. Not too long after I came home, he was in the Rio Grande Valley for a concert, and I was able to meet and visit with him for a while. I wanted to share my story with him because I wanted him to know that his songs touched my life and my family. They changed us. I encouraged him to keep on doing what he's doing.

The day of his concert my mom and I attended a "Greet and Meet" at the radio station. When he walked into the area where we were, he recognized me from the DVD about my story that my sister had sent him in an email. He walked over to me and said, "Wow! John you look great!" We visited and I shared with him how the lyrics, "I am fine except for the bump on my head," "I am not the man I used to be," and "God is not finished with me yet" really have special meaning for me. During the concert that night, he mentioned my name from the stage and called me his new friend. Afterwards, April and I went backstage to meet him and visit with him again. His music is making a difference.

Now that I am back home with my family, I am able to spend some time at the office and the gym each day. The way I look at it, you could say I was lucky or that God was on my side. I'm going to have to go with God was on my side.

When Mom told me that the therapists at TIRR said I needed to write a book and asked me what I thought about it, I said, "Sure, but everyone will need to put their part in because I really don't remember much; and if you leave it up to me, it will be the shortest book ever written."

My accident was bigger than anything our families had ever walked through, but the Lord never gives us more than we can handle. So, as a family, we wrote this book to encourage others not to give up or quit no matter what difficult or impossible circumstances come their way. I am living proof that miracles do happen today.

Early on, some of the medical records referred to me as an "unfortunate male involved in a motorcycle accident." I hope that this book helps you understand that traumatic brain injuries or any other type of situation like this are not hopeless. As long as you look to the Great Physician for healing, you can achieve anything. The Lord knew my outcome would be complete healing and restoration.

Through the power of prayer and miracles, he used my family, friends and community to help usher in my healing. My family is so remarkable, and I will never take them for granted again. They all took a year out of their lives to watch over me and fight for me, while I couldn't.

I love my wife, April, with my whole heart, and I want to thank her for staying by my side and helping me to find my way home again. I can't even imagine what it was like for her to take care of me and our precious boys all those months in Houston and then traveling back and forth to McAllen. She never quit, and she pushed me forward every step of the way. I, also, want to thank April's family for giving your love and time, helping take care of the boys and lending your hands and hearts to April when she needed you most.

To my dad and my mom, there are not words enough to express my love and gratitude for taking care of me and my family while I was away. My dad is one of the best men I have ever known in my life, and my mom is priceless, like a precious jewel. I am so blessed to have my sisters and their husbands, Jennifer and Rex, and Jené and Jon, and my brother Charles, who traveled to be with me countless times during this journey. My best friend, Robert, who had my back and watched over me, and my co-workers, Erasmo and his wife, Maria, who stepped up to the plate and took over in the Company, as well as everyone else at the Company who went the extra mile while I was away - I would not have made it if it were not for all of your help and prayers.

Countless doctors, nurses, therapists, and techs that encouraged me and were so creative in helping me find my way back to perfect health, to all of you, I give my gratitude. Rick, my brother in the Lord, you have been my faithful rock helping me return to health and strength since coming home.

Finally, the people that prayed for me from home and around the world, whether they knew me or not, unselfishly standing in the gap for me – your prayers were heard in heaven and have been answered. My mom said one time, "John, it took a whole community to raise you up!" My answer to that is, "Thank you, God, for Your people that hear Your voice and pray!"

I take every opportunity to tell everyone about what God did for me, whether it is in line at a store or speaking at churches or meetings. I can't stop talking about God's love and power to heal and to save. I will never stop praising the Lord and rejoicing over the miracle that I am and the great things He has done. I know the reason I am alive is because of God, and I give Him all the glory!

Miracle Testimony

Walter Keller

I am John's grandfather. When I got the call on Sunday afternoon from James about John's accident, I immediately proceeded to the hospital and met the rest of the family. We began to pray as a group as we waited for the ambulance to arrive. I thank God that no one ever gave up on John and that we all continued to believe for John's healing and recovery. I am so thankful for April and Jan as they never left John's side. I am grateful for all the doctors and their staff as they did all they could do for John. I will be forever thankful for my pastor and all my friends and church friends and all the churches that prayed for John. It blesses my heart when I consider all the people around the world I have never met that prayed for John. I am forever thankful for my family and all the families that prayed for John's healing and recovery. And most of all I thank God for what He has done for us in giving John back to us. I love you John.

Papa John

Epilogue

James Keller

The second anniversary of John's accident is fast approaching, and I must say that the last two years have been both the most challenging and the most rewarding years we have ever experienced. The phrase, "Tomorrow, about this time, things are going to change," has come full circle. From the time of the accident to the time of John walking out of the hospital in January 2009 to now another year later, that phrase continues to ring true. Things have changed, and it is wonderful to see what has happened.

John is the vice-president of Star Operators, Inc. and is in charge of 37 convenient stores and over 350 employees. His retail expertise is remarkable. He has the gift of always being able to figure it out, whatever "it" might be at that time. His tenacity to compete and win in this industry kept him focused and alert. John has always been quick to make decisions and move forward.

As I watch him today, he continues to be focused and has the gift of being able to figure "it" out. His insight and knowledge are moving him forward as that same competitive spirit drives him to compete. Today, John is determined to be 110% better than he was before the accident. Our God is faithful and just to complete the work He begins and He is doing this for John.

John's competitive spirit is pushing him forward in his vision and goals for the future. Recently, I saw it in action when John accepted a challenge to compete with a group of young men doing "push-ups" at a Fellowship of Christian Athlete's meeting where he had been invited to speak. John was on the floor doing "push-ups" and keeping up with or at times ahead of all those young men. Most of the others had dropped out, but John never missed a beat. His shirt was soaked with sweat when I reached down to give him a hand up. I asked him how many he had done, and he said he lost count. Our God is so awesome!

Recently, as we were completing the manuscript for this book, Margie Knight, our co-author, and I were exchanging emails about a message my friend, Chuck Pierce, had taught at Glory of Zion that morning. Here is what Margie forwarded to me:

> Listening to Chuck, there was so much revelation and confirmation about how John and all of you obtained the miracle of John's recovery as seen in these points:

> 1. You all endured your faith test in order to step into John's "new."

2. You "chose" to believe and went beyond where you were and allowed the Lord to extend your promise into the next season.

3. You didn't miss any connections with people and divine appointments.

4. You watched and recognized new forms of manifestations as you recognized key faith sign posts along the way, i.e. bill boards, sign outside Baptist church, sign over John's bed, etc. as confirmations.

5. You never hesitated to create a disturbance as you repeatedly said to everyone who would listen: Come & See! There Will be a Manifestation! Believe!

6. You received revelation that was beyond your ability in the natural to comprehend at the time, i.e. the doctors said he wouldn't walk or talk or live a normal life.

7. You warred over every prophetic word that came forth.

8. Your faith produced favor that set John apart for the future.

9. You aligned your time with His perfect time for the manifestation of John's healing. You didn't quit or give up no matter how many months it took.

10. You kept yearning and plowing until you could see the manifestation of your vision for John's healing.

But most significantly what I saw this morning from what Chuck said was that you were able to "SEE" the Road to Recovery and gain a new wind to advance!!! Chuck went on to say, "Vision will not be stopped in a time of seeing.'[1]"

From this statement and the points from Chuck's teaching, the title of John's book, *A Miracle on the Road to Recovery,* was confirmed in our hearts. It is our desire to help others be able to "SEE their road to recovery and gain a new wind." Miracles DO happen and we are standing with you for your miracle to manifest in God's perfect timing. We encourage you to implement the principles we utilized in Chuck's teaching listed above to bring your miracle forward into your present. God bless you on the journey!

Letter to John

Denny and Marty McGuire

February 6, 2010

Dear John,

There is a saying that, "Everyone must die but not everyone lives." In you, we see a young man who almost died but is now totally alive. We see a young man who knows the absolute commitment of his wife, family and friends, the reality of God and the power of prayer. We also see a young man who is much more aware of and in love with people - a young man who knows how truly precious life is.

John, you are a young man who has many years of life to lead your family and touch the world. As we think of your years to come I Cor. 2:9 NIV comes to mind, "*No eye has seen, no ear has heard, no mind has conceived what God has prepared for those who love Him.*" Psalm 147:10 NIV says, "*His pleasure is not in the strength of the horse, nor his delight in the legs of man; the Lord delights in those who fear him, who put their hope in his unfailing love.*"

John, never forget that you have already been blessed much more than most millionaires. You have, also, been a great blessing to us personally and to our entire family – thank you!

Love,

Denny and Marty McGuire

End Notes

Prologue

[1] Garlington, Joseph Dr., *Tomorrow About This Time Something is Going to Change, 2008.*

[2] Garlington, J. ibid.

[3] Pierce, Chuck. Starting the Year Off Right Conference, Glory of Zion International. 2008

Chapter 4

[1] http://en.wikipedia.org/wiki/Intracranial_hypertension

[2] http://en.wikipedia.org/wiki/Mannitol

Chapter 5

[1] http://dictionary.reference.com/browse/action

Chapter 10

[1] http://www.memorialhermann.org/locations/tirr/content.aspx?id=904

Chapter 12

[1] http://vic.australis.com.au/hazz/number005.html

Chapter 13

[1] http://www.neurosurgery.pitt.edu/pediatric/spasticity/baclofen_
spasticity.html

Epilogue

[1] Pierce, Chuck. Message "Changing the Way We Gather" at Glory of
Zion Outreach, January 24, 2010.

Author Bio

John C. Keller is a living testimony of God's power to heal and overcome death itself. After a life-threatening motorcycle crash in which he sustained a severe traumatic brain injury, John defied the odds 338 days later when he left the hospital walking and talking and praising the Lord.

As vice-president and CEO of Star Operations, Inc. in McAllen, Texas; John Keller directs 37 convenience stores and manages over 350 employees. His retail expertise and leadership guidance have resulted in the company being recognized by Shell Oil as a top performer with average Customer Value Bonus scores of over 96 out of 100. Star Operations gives back to the community by supporting Make A Wish Foundation, Fellowship of Christian Athletes and other school programs.

John holds a Bachelor of Arts degree in marketing from Texas A&M, Class of 1998. He is a graduate of Memorial High School in McAllen, TX. John resides in McAllen with his wife, April, and two sons, Caden and Dalton.

Co-Author Bio

For more than 20 years Margie Knight has been turning dreams into accomplished goals. Margie believes she is called to be a "servant to the servants of the Lord" and is gifted in capturing the anointing and style of authors as she writes and edits their work. *KnightWriter~2~Publish* is the Lord's vehicle to utilize her gifts for His kingdom as she helps others reach a higher level of success in their own kingdom callings.

With its complete turnkey approach to writing, editing, cover and interior design and publishing; *KnightWriter~2~Publish* offers the services needed to turn an author's ideas or manuscript into a quality product.

With more than 25 book projects successfully completed, *KnightWriter~2~Publish* commits to total customer satisfaction for every project. Margie says, *"Your goals are our goals as we match your vision to bring you success."*

For more information contact Margie Knight at:
KnightWriter2publish@gmail.com

Additional Information

To view updates on John's blog, go to:
www.johnkellerupdate.blogspot.com.

To view these videos:
John Keller: A Miracle in Progress
John Keller: From Miracle to Man
For the Kellers: With Love
go to www.youtube.com or google "John Keller"
and select the videos by name.

To order additional copies of:
A Miracle on the Road to Recovery
go to: www.johnkellerupdate.blogspot.com